Green Profits: The Budding Entrepreneur's Guide to a Houseplant Side Hustle

FINN ARBOR

Copyright © 2024 Snowdrift Homestead Publishing

All rights reserved.

ISBN: 979-8-9901387-0-4

DEDICATION

This book is dedicated to the entrepreneurial spirit that resides in the heart of each one of us—the dreamers, the doers, the relentless pursuers, inspired to transform the ordinary into something extraordinary. May the pages within inspire you to nurture your own ideas into reality.

Green Profits: The Budding Entrepreneur's Guide to a Houseplant Side Hustle

Green Profits: The Budding Entrepreneur's Guide to a Houseplant Side Hustle

CONTENTS

1	The Seed of an Idea	1
2	Sprouting Up on eBay and Etsy	8
3	Green Beginnings: Selecting and Adding Plants	19
4	Growing Strong: The Right Environment and Troubleshooting	31
5	Cuttings to Cash: Propagating Your Way to Profit	49
6	The Gardener's Toolkit: Essentials for a Flourishing Side Hustle	59
7	Branching Out: Business Structure and Legal Considerations	64
8	A Garden of Options for Selling Plants	73
9	From Green Leaves to Greenbacks: Houseplant Pricing	77
10	From Seed to Box: Secure and Effective Houseplant Shipping	82
11	Cultivating a Dream: Setting Goals and Creating a Business Plan	93
12	From Soil to Sale: Understanding and Defining Your Houseplant Niche	103
13	Photosynthesis of Ideas: Building a Marketing Plan	116
14	Unlocking a Digital Garden: Building a Website and More	121
15	Rooting a Presence: Website Design Meets Marketing Strategy	126
16	Turning New Leaves: Learning to Pivot	137
17	Growing Pains Begin and Partnerships Form	145
18	Green Spaces: The Next Big Expansion	149
19	Branching Out: Subscription Service Model	156
20	Dreams Continue to Grow	159

DISCLAIMER

The information provided in this book, " Green Profits: The Budding Entrepreneur's Guide to a Houseplant Side Hustle," is for general informational and educational purposes only. The author and publisher of this book make no representations or warranties of any kind, express or implied, about the completeness, accuracy, reliability, suitability, or availability with respect to the content contained on these pages for any purpose. Any reliance you place on such information is therefore strictly at your own risk.

The author and publisher are not engaged in rendering professional services, and this book is not a substitute for the advice of a legal, financial, or professional expert. The strategies and tips mentioned in this book are the author's personal opinions and should be taken as such. Readers should conduct their own research and due diligence and are encouraged to consult with a professional advisor for specific advice tailored to their situation.

The author and publisher shall not be liable for any loss, damage, or any other kind of liability from the use of this book, including but not limited to indirect or consequential loss or damage, any loss or damage whatsoever arising from loss of data or profits arising out of, or in connection with, the use of this book.

The success of your houseplant side hustle depends on various personal factors, market conditions, and other elements that may not be covered in this book. Therefore, the author and publisher do not guarantee that you will achieve results similar to those mentioned in case studies or examples in this book. You are solely responsible for your actions and results in life and business, which are dependent on personal factors including, but not limited to, your skill, knowledge, ability, dedication, business savvy, network, and financial situation.

By using this book, you agree to take full responsibility for your own results and to not hold the author or publisher accountable for any failure or lack of success. You understand that the author and publisher are providing valuable information, but that your success is ultimately up to you and the actions you take.

INTRODUCTION

Welcome to "Green Profits: The Budding Entrepreneur's Guide to a Houseplant Side Hustle," a book that introduces the entrepreneurial spirit of a side hustler to the world of houseplants. This book is a blend of storytelling and business strategy, intended to provide practical advice to help you transform a love of plants into a thriving business.

The idea behind this book is straightforward: it is possible to turn a love of raising and selling houseplants from a hobby to a side hustle, or even full-time business.

In this story you'll meet Lily, a green-thumb fanatic who transforms her passion for houseplants into a successful business. But this is more than just a story; it's a practical guide that you can use to begin profiting from your own houseplant hobby.

The lessons we'll draw from Lily's experiences are as real as the soil her plants grow in. In these pages, you'll find a relatable and engaging roadmap to success. From understanding your target market to selecting houseplants, from navigating the logistics of online platforms to the nuances of customer care and business partnerships – in each chapter new lessons and actionable steps unfold, guiding you to grow your very own venture from the ground up.

So, whether you're already a houseplant enthusiast who is looking to generate extra income, or someone with no houseplant experience who is seeking a unique, viable, low start-up cost side hustle in a growing market, this book is for you.

1 THE SEED OF AN IDEA

Let me introduce you to Lily whose journey started in bustling Denver, Colorado. Lily was always known among her group of close friends for her small but lush urban jungle, a collection of houseplants that thrived in her apartment even while snow fell on the other side of the window. Each day, after returning from her uninspiring office job, Lily found solace tending to her green friends.

One early spring day, while pruning her plants, and appreciating the healthy new growth that she observed, an idea sparked. She carefully snipped off cuttings from a couple plants with new growth, being sure to cut just above a node as her grandmother had long ago taught her. She placed her new cuttings in water and nurtured them in the days that followed. Soon, the tiny cuttings had grown roots and leaves of their own.

With roots and leaves growing, Lily repotted the young plants and gifted one to her friend Sally who had always gushed about how beautiful Lily's plants were and how she wished that she too had a living room full of plants. Sally loved her new plant and couldn't wait to bring it home.

A couple of weeks later, Sally called Lily. She shared that her mother's birthday was right around the corner, and she asked Lily if she would be willing to sell another plant. Lily was flattered that someone wanted to give one of her plants as a gift. Sally suggested that they look on Etsy and eBay for similar plant offerings to align on a fair market price. And with that, Lily's eyes had been opened.

That evening, Lily couldn't stop searching eBay, Etsy, Craigslist, and Facebook Marketplace. She was astonished to see that people were actually taking cuttings of their houseplants, rooting them and growing them into young plants that they were offering for sale – and the plants were selling!

Lily's interest began to quickly transition from houseplant hobbyist to entrepreneur. She had always valued feeling connected to nature and the sense of tranquility that she found while tending to her plants helped fulfill that need. The prospect of sharing this joy with others was exhilarating!

As Lily thought more and more about the idea of a houseplant side hustle, she felt like it was something she would be able to navigate with relative ease because it dovetailed so seamlessly into her existing lifestyle. The flexibility of being able to manage plant care and sales during her free time meant she wouldn't have to choose between her day job and her passion – she could cultivate them both simultaneously.

Moreover, this venture seemed like it would have low start-up costs, making it possible for her to jump right in. She already possessed the fundamental knowledge and materials she needed to propagate her plants. The cuttings from her own houseplants were essentially free stock, and the initial overhead costs—maybe at first just a couple pots and another bag of soil—would be minimal. This made the venture feel less risky and simply like a natural, organic extension of her existing hobby.

Houseplant Side Hustle Opportunities

You are about to embark on a journey where you'll be invited to join Lily and others like her who have discovered that with the right care, dedication, and knowledge, a side hustle in houseplants can bloom into a life-changing pursuit. Lily's story is a testament to the magic that can happen when passion meets perseverance.

Over the pages of this book, you'll hear how Lily turned her love for houseplants into a thriving business, transforming her financial future, while spreading her love for plants far and wide. Her plants continue to grow in many homes across the country, and so does her legacy, one leaf at a time.

We'll check back in with Lily throughout this book, but let's begin our journey together by examining the rise of the houseplant hobby that makes this venture possible.

The Rise of the Houseplant Hobby

Houseplants have seen a surge in popularity, largely due to shifts in lifestyle that were brought on by the increase in remote work that began to boom during the COVID-19 pandemic. People suddenly found themselves needing to design home offices that could be pleasant and calming to be in, and that could also serve as backdrops for remote webcam meetings. For many, houseplants fit the bill as the perfect way to beautify their space and help them find solace in a home office.

Plants are uniquely able to improve both a room's aesthetic and air quality, which is important when you're spending many hours in the same space. There's a growing awareness of just how important indoor air quality is, and plants promise the added benefits of absorbing toxins and producing oxygen. As people work to make their homes healthier, this natural houseplant benefit contributes to the surge in popularity.

Houseplants offer others a way to bring nature indoors. Millions of people live in urban areas with limited access to outdoor green spaces. For those living in apartments or homes without gardens, indoor plants can satisfy a natural desire to connect with nature.

Social media platforms like Instagram and Pinterest continue contributing to the popularity of houseplants, enabling people to showcase their beautifully curated interiors, filled with lush greenery. Influencers and plant enthusiasts are everywhere, sharing their plant collections, care tips, and stunning plant-filled rooms, all the while inspiring others to start their own collections.

These factors have not only increased the popularity of houseplants but have also opened the potential for a range of supporting entrepreneurial ventures, like our friend Lily is discovering. As people seek to beautify their homes with greenery, learn more about plant care, and connect with others who share their interests, the market for houseplants and related products will continue to grow.

Is a Houseplant Side Hustle Right for You?

Raising and selling houseplants can be an attractive option for anyone with a passion for plants, who is looking for a flexible source of income, and interested in capitalizing on the growing demand for indoor greenery. Whether it's a hobby turned business or a strategic income generating venture, a houseplant side hustle offers many benefits and opportunities for personal, professional, and financial fulfillment. Let's look at some of the reasons why a houseplant side hustle might be right for you.

Flexibility

A houseplant business is an appealing and flexible side hustle option. It's easy to pursue this type of entrepreneurial ambition while maintaining your current employment. It's an ideal business model for anyone who needs to make sure their side project can peacefully coexist with other obligations.

Raising and selling houseplants is a relatively easy way to supplement your income, without requiring you to commit to the long hours of a typical job or a more demanding side business. The work to maintain and grow your houseplant business can be done at your own pace. Unlike a regular 9 to 5 job or taking on a second job to boost your income, a houseplant side hustle can be tailored to fit into the nooks and crannies of your day. Whether you're an early riser who gets energy in the morning or a night owl who finds energy after the sun sets, this is a business that can, generally speaking, be adapted to your natural patterns.

Low Startup Costs

Another benefit of starting a houseplant side hustle is that the initial capital requirements are typically minimal compared to many other business ventures. It is possible to get started on an extremely small scale, making this an accessible option for nearly anyone.

Even better, the ongoing financial demands of this business are also minimal. Sunlight, water, and some basic care are often all that's needed for plants to thrive.

And, like Lily, you might already have a collection of healthy houseplants to get you started. For many of us it is possible to start today, simply by taking a couple cuttings off existing plants.

Dynamic Resources – Self-Propagating Assets

A unique and very appealing aspect of a houseplant side hustle is that houseplants are dynamic resources. Plants are a living, self-replenishing inventory that can be expanded through natural processes. With a little help, your houseplants can create new plants without needing you to make ongoing, expensive inventory re-purchases. Imagine running a business where the inventory was capable of self-replication – that is exactly what houseplants offer! This somewhat unique aspect of the houseplant business model makes it particularly attractive to those looking to start a low-risk side hustle, or for those with limited capital.

Value Increases with Time

Even better, given the right conditions, your plants will grow and increase in size and value without the need for continuous financial outlay.

It's true, as plants grow and mature, they typically become more valuable! A small cutting that may have been worth a few dollars initially, can, over time, grow into a large, lush plant that commands a much higher price.

Potential for Profit

With a little bit of planning and effective marketing, raising and selling houseplants can be a profitable endeavor. There's a diverse market for houseplants that includes collectors, interior designers, and individuals seeking to enhance their living space with greenery. Houseplants also make wonderful gifts, further expanding the market potential.

The interest in houseplants spans demographics. What is interesting to note is that demand for houseplants has seen a particular surge among millennials and Gen Z, who often share their plant collections on social media. These age groups also just so happen to be more likely to live in urban environments with limited outdoor space, increasing their desire for houseplants to bring nature indoors.

Health and Wellness Trends

The wellness industry has embraced houseplants as a way to improve indoor air quality and promote mental well-being. The purported health benefits of houseplants, such as reducing stress and improving air quality, align with growing consumer focus on health and wellness, particularly in the aftermath of the pandemic.

Interior Design and Aesthetics

Houseplants have become a significant element in interior design, with architects and designers incorporating green spaces into their plans. Consumers are investing in houseplants not only for their health benefits but also for their ability to enhance living spaces, which has been important as homes have doubled as offices and recreational spaces.

E-Commerce Platforms Make Customers Accessible

We live in an amazing time where it's possible to reach a nationwide, or even worldwide, customer base from the comfort of home. E-commerce platforms such as Etsy and eBay have become booming houseplant marketplaces that allow you to easily reach a wide audience. Specialty plant shops and larger e-commerce platforms have expanded their offerings, and social media marketplaces have also facilitated the trade and sale of plants.

With a few considerations, it is incredibly easy to get started in this business, simply by creating listings today for your houseplants or cuttings on popular e-commerce sites, like eBay and Etsy.

Using these platforms does require you to learn a bit about how to take create an effective listing and how to take compelling photographs of your plants, but for most houseplant sellers, the ability to significantly expand your target market to eBay and/or Etsy buyers is well worth the learning curve.

2 SPROUTING UP ON EBAY AND ETSY

The day Lily realized that it was possible to sell houseplants and cuttings on eBay and Etsy, she was hooked!

Lily immediately walked around her apartment, examining each of her plants and assessing which ones were healthy and had sufficient new growth to sustain a cutting. She got to work starting her cuttings and posted her first few online listings. Her initial start was modest, two cuttings from her beloved Monstera Deliciosa and six offsets that her prolific curly spider plant was all too eager to create.

She was surprised at the response; the cuttings sold out in no time! Her six curly spider plant babies sold for $6 each and she was able to sell the two Monstera Deliciosa cuttings for $12 apiece. In her first week, Lily had sold $60 worth of plants, simply by sharing cuttings taken from just two of her many houseplants.

This became a weekly ritual. Lily would propagate one or two cuttings from different plants in her collection, nurture them, and post them online. If not all cuttings in a week sold, she would simply let them keep growing. She would then sell them as small potted plants, which she found commanded an even higher price point!

She learned some tips and tricks to improve her listings during these early months, as she focused on creating compelling content and taking beautiful pictures of her plants.

Creating Compelling Online Listings

Creating an engaging and informative online listing is key to successfully selling houseplants. Buyers are seeking basic information and there are several key elements you should consider including in online descriptions to make your listings stand out and appeal to potential buyers.

A good listing includes both the common and botanical name of the plant. This is an easy way to help you avoid confusion or disappointed customers, due to potential regional variations in common plant names. Including the botanical name also elevates your perceived expertise as a houseplant seller and allows you to cater to both casual buyers and more knowledgeable enthusiasts. Providing both the common and botanical names allows customers to conduct further research into the plant, empowering them to access a wealth of information from various sources, such as botanical gardens, horticultural resources, or plant care guides. This can contribute to your customers' ultimate success by giving them access to information they need in order to provide optimal care and to their houseplants.

A good listing for a plant or cutting also details the current size of the plant (height and spread), and sets expectations for its potential growth size, if the plant is cared for properly. Additionally, information on the growth rate can help your customers understand how much time will be required for their plant to reach its mature size.

By offering detailed care instructions, including light requirements (e.g., indirect light, full sun), how frequently the plant needs to be watered, its humidity preferences and temperature range, buyers can better assess whether they can provide a suitable environment. Also consider offering practical care tips and maintenance advice in your listings. This might include guidance on pruning, fertilizing, repotting, and any other specific considerations for maintaining the plant's health and appearance.

Seasonal Considerations

Highlight any seasonal considerations for the plant and its care. This could include flowering periods, dormancy, or specific care adjustments that the plant might need during different seasons.

Potting Information

Mention whether the plant will be shipped in its pot or if it will be shipped bare root. If it comes with a pot, describe the type of pot material (e.g., ceramic, plastic) and its size.

Health and Condition

Describe the current health and condition of the plant, noting any unique features or if it's flowering. Be honest about any imperfections to set the right expectations.

Shipping Information

Clearly state your shipping policies. Include information about how you will package the plant, the carriers you use, estimated delivery times, and regions you ship to. Mention if you offer combined shipping for multiple purchases.

We'll cover more about shipping, including regulatory restrictions related to the shipment of houseplants in greater detail later in this book. But for the time being, it's important to understand that there are restrictions that regulate the importation of plants and plant products to the following states: California, Florida, Arizona, Hawaii and Texas. For a beginner selling houseplants online, it's recommended that your listing note you are not able to ship to these states.

Return Policy

Your listing should also outline your return policy in case the plant arrives damaged or significantly different from the description. Will you reship a replacement plant? Will you offer refunds for plants or cuttings that do not survive the shipping journey? Answering these questions proactively can help buyers understand what to expect and become comfortable purchasing from you.

Special Features or Benefits

If there are any special features of the plant you are offering, such as air-purifying qualities, ease of care, or rarity, these can be very valuable to highlight in your listing.

Plant history or background might not always be information you have available, but wherever possible, include in your description interesting information about the plant's origin. This could be about the history of the plant, or a related story. This can make your listing more engaging and personal and help differentiate you from other online houseplant sellers.

Indicate whether the plant is suitable for beginners or if it requires more advanced care. This will help your customers make informed decisions based on their experience level.

Responses to Frequently Asked Questions (FAQs)

Anticipate and answer common questions you might receive about the plant, such as if it's pet-friendly, how often it flowers, or how to repot it. Include this information in an FAQ section of your listing.

By including comprehensive and informative details in your online houseplant listing descriptions, you'll greatly enhance the appeal of your plants. Including these elements helps you proactively provide essential information to buyers, and ultimately contributes to a better customer experience. Your customers will be able to make informed purchasing decisions and feel confident in their plant selections.

Compelling Plant Photographs

High-quality images from multiple angles are crucial. Photos in with your listings should include close-ups of leaves and flowers, if applicable, and possibly a photo of your plants next to a common object for scale.

You don't have to be a professional photographer to take compelling photos that draw in potential buyers. Browse other eBay or Etsy listings to understand the types of photos that are helping others sell their plants. You'll quickly find that an online seller of houseplants and cuttings can use a variety of pictures, and even videos, to effectively showcase their plants and draw in customers.

Here are some types of visual content that can help an online seller of houseplants and cuttings engage potential customers, build trust, and effectively showcase their products.

High-Quality Pictures

You will want to take clear, high-resolution images of individual plants. This will help your customers get a good look at each plant's size, shape, and overall condition. Close-up shots of any unique features, such as foliage patterns or blooms can also be appealing.

The best part is you don't even need a fancy camera to take effective pictures. For most of us, a smartphone camera, and a willingness to experiment with lighting and different angles is all it takes. Over time, as your business expands, you may want to invest in a lightbox or other camera equipment, but special equipment is not necessary to get started.

Lifestyle Images

Showcasing plants in real-life settings, such as a well-decorated living room, office space, or on a balcony, can help customers envision how the plants will look in their own environments. Lifestyle images evoke emotions and create a desire to own the plants.

Consider staging plant photographs to showcase how the plant can elevate your customers' living space. For customers who are discovering houseplants through a primary interest in interior design, lifestyle images are especially impactful.

Plant Care Tutorials

Videos or images that demonstrate plant care tips, such as watering, repotting, and pruning, can provide valuable information to customers and build trust in your expertise. This type of content can also help customers feel more confident in their ability to care for the plants they purchase.

Brief tutorial images can be especially impactful for sellers who are interested in catering to a beginner focused houseplant market.

Unboxing Videos

Short videos that demonstrate what a buyer can expect when they receive their plant are highly effective. Consider creating videos that show the unboxing experience of receiving a plant or cutting to help build excitement and anticipation for your customer.

Unboxing videos can also showcase the quality of your packaging and reinforce the care you take when shipping plants.

Importantly, for customers who have never purchased a plant online and had it shipped to them, unboxing videos can help them understand what to expect and can alleviate potential questions or concerns.

Before and After Pictures

Sharing before and after images of plants, particularly if you are selling cuttings or young plants, can help set initial customer expectations and build excitement. Pictures that show young plants growing and thriving under a customer's care can demonstrate the potential of the plants and encourage others to make a purchase.

These can also help ensure your customer understands

that they are receiving a young plant, and only with the right care and time will it grow into its lush "after" stage. This can help avoid potential negative reviews if a customer sees a picture of a mature plant and doesn't read the description to understand they are buying a smaller cutting.

Customer Testimonials

Over time, sharing images or videos of customers satisfied with their purchased plants, along with their testimonials, can build social proof and trust in your products.

As your business expands and you have positive reviews under your belt, consider enriching your listings with screenshots of happy five-star reviews, photos or videos that tell your story through the voice of past customers.

Educational Content

Photos and videos that educate customers about plant varieties, care requirements, and propagation techniques can help position you as a knowledgeable resource and can help customers make informed purchasing decisions.

Behind-the-Scenes Content

Providing a glimpse into your greenhouse, propagation process, or plant care routines can humanize your brand and help you create a deep connection with customers.

Continuous Improvement - Learning from Online Reviews

An aspiring online seller of houseplants and cuttings can learn valuable insights from the positive and negative reviews left for other houseplant sellers. By leveraging the insights gained from competitor reviews, you'll be able to refine your products, product descriptions, and service offerings to address customer needs and stand out in the market.

This proactive approach can create a differentiated brand

and customer-centric business that attracts and retains a loyal following. Here are some things to think about as you scan reviews left for other sellers:

Identify Common Pain Points

By analyzing negative reviews, you can identify recurring issues or complaints houseplant customers have. In general, these include problems with plant quality, packaging, lengthy shipping times, inaccurate descriptions, or customer service challenges.

Understanding these pain points can help you proactively address similar potential issues in your own offerings and provide solutions that differentiate you from competitors.

Highlight Strengths and Unique Selling Points

Positive reviews reveal the strengths and unique selling points that houseplant customers appreciate. Happy houseplant customers often leave reviews touting exceptional plant quality, personalized service, and informative product descriptions.

Identify Gaps in the Market

Negative reviews can also help you identify gaps or unmet needs in the market that you may be able to capitalize on.

For example, if customers complain about receiving limited information about how to care for their plants, you can use this feedback to begin providing comprehensive care guides with your plants, setting you apart.

Improve Customer Service

Understanding the service-related feedback from competitor reviews can help you enhance your own customer service. Whether it's responding to inquiries promptly, being prepared to provide personalized recommendations, or offering post-purchase plant care support, you can use feedback that has been publicly shared about other sellers' shortcomings to improve your customer service expectation.

Keeping Negative Feedback in Perspective

It happens. You do everything you can to select healthy plants, accurately describe what you are selling, securely package and ship your plant. Nonetheless, you'll occasionally receive negative customer feedback. Managing negative feedback and keeping it in perspective is crucial for your business's growth. Live plants are a higher risk category. You're going to experience carrier delays when shipping your products, extreme weather during shipment and other factors outside your control. It happens to everyone who sells online at some point, and there are strategies to help you effectively handle negative feedback.

By being financially prepared to occasionally refund orders and learning not to take negative feedback personally you'll be equipped to learn from negative feedback and continually improve.

Quality Control Focused Feedback

Perhaps a buyer left feedback that a plant you sent was wilting or had brown spots or dead leaves. These point to quality control opportunities for your business. By analyzing what went wrong and implementing more stringent quality control measures, you can minimize the risk of future issues. Learning how to treat pest infestations, disease, and how to protect your plants from damage during shipping will be a continual journey. Conduct thorough inspections before shipping to ensure that only healthy plants are sent to customers.

Accurate Product Representation

If a customer leaves feedback that they thought they were receiving a bigger plant based on the listing, or otherwise are concerned that the plant received didn't match the description, you probably have opportunities to improve your listing descriptions.

Oftentimes in the houseplant online market, this type of feedback will crop up when a seller takes pictures of only their mother plant. Buyers making quick purchasing decisions could be disappointed to receive a cutting or small start. Providing detailed and accurate descriptions of the plants, including size, condition, and growth habits is key. If you are selling cuttings, ensure your listing clearly explains this, and that the pictures included in your listing also include pictures of the cutting – not just your thriving mother plant. Consider taking pictures that present a visual comparison of the actual plant to a common household item, like a dollar bill or a can of soda.

Clear Communication

Set clear expectations with customers regarding the nature of live plants, their care requirements, and the potential for variations in appearance due to natural growth patterns. Provide comprehensive care instructions and guidelines to help your customers acclimatize their plant upon arrival.

Responsive Customer Service

Maintain open lines of communication with your customers and promptly address any concerns or issues that arise. Most times, a buyer will contact you before leaving a negative review. This is an opportunity for you to offer solutions such as replacements, refunds, or care advice to mitigate dissatisfaction and build trust.

Proactive Problem-Solving

Monitor for any patterns or recurring issues you see in negative feedback and take steps to address underlying problems, such as adjusting shipping methods or improving packaging.

A good example of proactive problem-solving is specifying that you only ship plants during certain weekdays to avoid plants potentially sitting at a post office facility on a Sunday.

You also can consider learning from feedback and offering friendly post-sale outreach to help your customers understand how best to care for their new plant and to address questions or challenges they might be having.

Continuous Improvement

Ultimately, all feedback is a gift. Use negative feedback as an opportunity for personal growth and business improvement. Regularly review customer feedback and identify areas for enhancement in product quality, customer service, and overall customer experience.

3 GREEN BEGINNINGS: SELECTING AND ADDING PLANTS

Enjoying her early success as a houseplant entrepreneur, Lily decided to strategically expand her plant collection. She wasn't just a plant lover anymore; she was a plant entrepreneur, and every addition to her collection was a step towards expanding her business. She had been monitoring other plant sales online and started a list of plants that she dreamt about adding. It was time to learn more about each plant and make decisions.

First on her list was the Fiddle Leaf Fig which she found to be absolutely striking. Its towering presence and glossy leaves had made it a staple in interior design magazines, and Lily knew it would be a valuable addition. As she poured over online resources and plant books, she realized that caring for the Fiddle Leaf Fig required a bit more attention than many of her existing plants. It thrived in indirect light and needed consistent moisture without waterlogging, which meant that well-draining soil and a careful watering schedule would be crucial.

Lily also decided to add a collection of succulents, including the Echeveria and the Zebra Plant (Haworthia). These low-maintenance beauties were perfect for her beginner customers and offered an attractive margin due to their ease of propagation and care. Succulents required minimal watering, thriving in dry conditions with plenty of light, and could easily be propagated from leaves or cuttings, making them an efficient choice for her growing business.

Another strategic addition was the Snake Plant (Sansevieria), popular for its air-purifying qualities and almost indestructible nature. It could thrive in low-light conditions and requires infrequent watering, appealing to a wide range of customers, from busy professionals to those new to plant care. Lily also liked that this plant thrived in low lighting because space in her apartment was limited. A plant that needed less light wouldn't be competing for her already limited window-front space. Lily also liked that it could be easily propagated through division. In the end, for her business, she saw the Snake Plant as a low-effort, high-reward option.

With each new plant, Lily meticulously documented the care requirements, creating a resource she could refer back to and eventually share with her customers. By offering healthy, well-cared-for plants and sharing her knowledge on how to maintain them, Lily knew she could build trust and loyalty with her customers.

With careful research, strategic selections, and a lot of love, Lily was nurturing her dream, one plant at a time, laying the groundwork for what she now hoped would grow into a thriving houseplant empire.

Selecting Plants

Like Lily, you might find yourself wanting to add plants to your collection. You're likely also wondering, "How many houseplants would someone need to maintain a successful side hustle?" or "What types of houseplants are most profitable?" Let's dig deeper into these questions and other topics that are important when selecting plants for a houseplant side hustle.

So, how many houseplants would someone need to maintain a successful side hustle? It might not be the most satisfying answer, but the honest answer is, "It depends!" The number of houseplants needed to sustain a successful side hustle selling plants that you propagate is going to vary based on several factors, including the types of plants you plan to sell, how readily they propagate, market demand for those plants and the scale of your operation. Ultimately, the number of houseplants you will need will depend on your personal capacity, market demand, the plants you select and your specific goals for your business. Starting with a manageable number of plants and gradually expanding based on demand and resources is always a prudent approach.

Types of Plants to Consider

If your goal is creating a profitable venture, focusing on houseplants that are in demand, fetch a high selling price, and are relatively easy to propagate is a great strategy. Luckily there are many popular houseplants that check these boxes. This book is not a dictionary of all types of houseplants, there are plenty of other resources available if you're interested in a comprehensive review of all plant options. To start your research journey, here are twenty-five types of houseplants that have market appeal and tend to sell well.

1. **Monstera Deliciosa**, often commonly referred to as "Swiss Cheese Vine" or "Swiss Cheese Plant." These are highly sought after for their unique split leaves. Mature plants can sell for a significant markup, and simple cuttings (at the time this book was written) can sell online for $10 or more. If you are able to obtain a variegated variety, they can fetch an even higher price with cuttings of some variegated varieties selling for $55 or more, based on the type and extent of variegation. Another Monstera Deliciosa benefit is that they are easily propagated from stem cuttings that can be placed in either water or directly in soil.

2. **Ficus Lyrata**, often referred to as "Fiddle Leaf Fig" is another in demand high value houseplant. These plants are popular for their large, glossy leaves and

the visual impact they have on a space. Like all plants, larger specimens command high prices, though small starter plants can also fetch high prices. Most listings for Ficus Lyrata online are for small starter plants, rather than cuttings. These plants can be propagated from leaf or stem cuttings, but the process requires more patience than other plant varieties. If you're interested in selling young plants, starter plants are recommended versus attempting to sell as cuttings which could be frustrating for buyers, potentially leading to negative reviews and a poor customer experience.

3. **Epipremnum aureum**, commonly referred to as "Pothos," are in demand and sell well. These plants are known for their hardiness and ability to thrive in low light. There are a wide variety of options; so many, in fact, that some sellers offer variety boxes with multiple cuttings! Like other plants, variegated varieties, like "Golden Pothos" and "Marble Queen" command premium pricing. Even better, these plants are very easy to propagate from stem cuttings in water or soil.

4. **Sansevieria**, more commonly referred to as "Snake Plant" is valued for its air-purifying qualities and requires minimal care, helping it appeal to a wide audience, including both beginners and a health-conscious customer base. Rare varieties like "Sansevieria Trifasciata" can be quite lucrative. Sansevieria can be propagated through leaf cuttings or division; both methods are straightforward.

5. **Succulents**, across various genera, are always popular due to their tremendous variety and low maintenance. Rare species or those with unusual

colors or shapes command higher prices. Succulents are also generally easy to propagate from leaves, offsets, or stem cuttings, depending on the species.

6. **Zamioculcas zamiifolia**, or "ZZ Plant," is a fan favorite, thanks to its tolerance of neglect and low-light conditions. Mature, large plants can be sold for a good margin. This is another plant that is typically sold as a potted plant, ranging from young starter plants to larger, mature plants, rather than sold as cuttings. These plants can be propagated through division or leaf cuttings, though growth is typically slow.

7. **Philodendron** are sought after for their diverse foliage options and ease of care. Rare varieties like "Philodendron Pink Princess" are highly coveted. Propagation is also easy, with stem cuttings doing well in water or soil.

8. **Alocasia** or "Elephant Ear Plants" are known for their striking foliage and architectural presence. Some rare varieties can fetch extremely high prices. Propagation is typically done through rhizome division or offsets, depending on the species.

9. **Chlorophytum Comosum**, or "Spider Plants," are another great plant. There are multiple varieties, some such as "Bonnie Curly," "Zebra Grass," "Hawaiian" and variegated plants fetch higher prices. Sellers with multiple varieties in their collection often offer variety boxes of "pups" taken from multiple types of spider plants. Spider plants are known for their attractive leaves and easy care, making them a staple for both beginners and enthusiasts. These plants also propagate readily from "pups" or baby plants that form on long stems and can be potted

separately as soon as roots develop.

10. **Senecio Rowleyanus,** often referred to as "String of Pearls" offers unique bead-like leaves that make it a sought-after decorative plant, perfect for hanging baskets. They are easily propagated from cuttings, just lay them on top of the soil, and they'll root with minimal additional effort.

11. **Ficus Elastica**, common name "Rubber Plant," has large, glossy leaves, and is a statement piece for decorators. It's also known for its air-purifying qualities, giving it appeal with a health-conscious customer base as well. These plants can be propagated through leaf or stem cuttings in either water or soil, though they do require some patience.

12. **Crassula Ovata**, or "Jade Plant" is considered a symbol of good luck, making it a perfect plant to appeal to gift givers! It is easy to care for and very easy to propagate from leaves or stem cuttings; by simply placing the cuttings in soil they will typically root and grow well.

13. **Peperomia Varieties** are beloved for their diverse and ornamental foliage. They also are sought after for small spaces and fit well on desks. They can be propagated from leaf cuttings or by dividing small offshoots, which makes them easy to multiply.

14. **Maranta Leuconeura**, or "Prayer Plant" is known for striking leaf patterns and movement in response to light, which makes it a fascinating plant for collectors. It's another great plant to consider, as they are easy to propagate by dividing the root ball or by stem cuttings and placing them directly in soil or water.

15. **Pilea Peperomioides**, commonly called "Chinese Money Plant" has unique round leaves. They are also easy to care for, and a must-have plant in many collections. "Chinese Money Plants" propagate easily from pups that grow from the base of the plant. These pups can be separated and potted once they have a good root system.

16. **Hoya Varieties** are a perpetual favorite and in demand for their waxy leaves and beautiful, fragrant flowers. Varieties like Hoya kerrii ("Heart Hoya") are particularly popular. They're easy to propagate from stem cuttings in water or soil, making them easy to share and sell.

17. **Saintpaulia**, or "African Violet" are loved for their beautiful, velvety flowers in various colors. They come in a compact size, which makes them perfect for indoor spaces. These plants are easy to propagate from leaf cuttings placed in water or soil.

18. **Asplenium Nidus**, or "Bird's Nest Fern" is a beautiful plant with ripple-edged fronds, this fern adds a unique texture to indoor plant collections. It's also known for being more forgiving than other types of ferns. These plants can be propagated through spores or by dividing the plant at the base during repotting.

19. **Tradescantia zebrina**, commonly called "Wandering Dude" or "Wandering Jew" are striking plants with variegated leaves that make them a favorite for hanging baskets and decorative tabletops. They are extremely easy to propagate from stem cuttings placed in water or directly in soil.

20. **Nephrolepis exaltata**, or "Boston Fern" are popular

for lush, feathery fronds and air-purifying qualities. They are ideal for hanging baskets or as standalone plants and can be propagated by dividing the root ball when repotting.

21. **Spathiphyllum**, often referred to as "Peace Lily" are known for elegant white blooms and low-light tolerance, which make them a popular choice for indoor environments. They are typically propagated by dividing the root mass during repotting.

22. **Kalanchoe** plants offer appealing flowers and succulent leaves and are especially popular for those looking for low-maintenance blooms. Kalanchoe is also easy to propagate from leaf cuttings or by removing offsets.

23. **Syngonium**, or "Arrowhead Plant" is valued for its attractive foliage and versatility, as it can be grown as a trailing or climbing plant. They can also be easily propagated from stem cuttings placed in water or soil.

24. **Haworthiopsis Attenuate**, or "Zebra Plant" is a succulent known for its striking, striped leaves and ease of care, appealing to both beginners and enthusiasts. It's another easy to propagate option, doing well from either offsets or leaf cuttings.

25. **Hedera Helix**, known as "English Ivy" is a classic and versatile plant. It's ideal for hanging baskets or as a climbing vine and is also known for its air-purifying capabilities. These plants are very easy to propagate from stem cuttings placed in water or soil.

When starting your side hustle, consider focusing on a mix of plants like the ones detailed in this section, or others, that allow you to cater to different market segments and preferences. Of course, some houseplants propagate more readily than others. Fast growing, popular plants with high demand, such as pothos, spider plants, or succulents, can be more profitable for propagation because you are able to produce more. There's also great benefit to having a variety of plants with different propagation schedules, which can be a great technique to help ensure you have a steady supply for potential customers.

When selling plants online, it's important to highlight the level of care they require, any unique features, and any special instructions for propagation that might help you attract buyers. Researching popular trends and identifying sought after houseplant varieties can help you quantify your potential for sales, and from there, understand how many of that type of plant you would need to meet the expected market demand.

When selecting what types of plants to offer and how many you will choose to maintain, consider the space and resources that might be needed for the plants you choose. Adequate lighting and proper growing conditions are essential for successful propagation. Your existing space might influence the type of plants you choose to grow, as well as the size of your initial houseplant side hustle. Unfortunately, not all propagated plants will thrive. Maintaining a larger number of parent plants can help ensure you have a consistent supply of successful propagations available for sale.

Obtaining Suitable Parent Plants

If you do choose to add plants, there are many ways to source suitable parent plants. Of course, local nurseries or garden centers often have a wide variety of houseplants, including popular and unique species that could be used as parent plants for propagating new ones.

There are also many online plant retailers who offer a wide selection of houseplants that can be purchased and used for propagation. Some popular online plant retailers include The Sill, Bloomscape, and yes, eBay and Etsy. It is important to research and read reviews of any retailer you are considering, ensuring they have a good reputation for providing healthy plants and excellent customer service.

Plant swaps or local plant enthusiast groups can be another great way to connect with other plant lovers who may be willing to trade or sell cuttings to help you build your collection.

Regardless of where you choose to source your plants from, it is absolutely crucial that the plants you select are healthy and free from pests and diseases. This will help you protect your existing plants, and provide the best quality products to your customers.

Establishing a Bio Security Process

Establishing a bio security process to ensure you do not inadvertently introduce pests or disease to your existing plants when adding new plants is important. When adding a new plant, you should implement quarantine and sanitation protocols to keep new plants separate from your existing plants for a period of time. As your plant business grows, part of your bio security process should also include regularly inspecting your plants for signs of pests or disease.

Houseplants are susceptible to a wide range of pests and diseases that can quickly spread from one plant to another. Implementing bio security measures can help prevent the introduction and spread of these threats, protecting the health of your plants and the reputation of your business. A good bio security process also demonstrates your commitment to ethical and responsible plant care, which can enhance your reputation as a seller. It shows customers that you take plant health and environmental stewardship seriously, which can help build trust and loyalty.

Soil Sterilization

Did you know that soil can also harbor pests and diseases, which could devastate your plant inventory? It's true. One of the biggest steps you can take to protect your plants from harmful pests and disease is ensuring that you only use sterilized potting mix or that you treat your soil or growing medium. This is especially important for a houseplant entrepreneur looking to ensure the quality and health of their products. Luckily, there are multiple methods available to sterilize soil and help prevent future detrimental pest or disease problems.

You can sterilize your soil mixture by either baking or microwaving it. To sterilize soil in an oven, place moist soil on a baking tray and cover it with aluminum foil. Bake in the oven at 200-250°F (about 93-121°C) for about 30 minutes. The soil should reach an internal temperature of at least 180°F (82°C), which will kill most pathogens and pests. You will want to monitor the temperature closely to avoid burning the soil. Another option is microwaving your soil by putting about 2 pounds of moist soil in a microwave-safe bag. Leave the bag open and microwave on full power for 2 to 5 minutes, again until the middle of the soil reaches 180°F (82°C). Whether you sterilize soil in the oven or a microwave, let it cool before use.

If you have a large quantity of soil to sterilize, solarization may be a better option. This involves spreading soil in a thin layer sandwiched between two clear plastic sheets and leaving it in direct sunlight for 4-6 weeks, ideally during the hottest part of the year. The heat generated under the plastic will kill pests, pathogens, and weed seeds.

There are various chemical treatment sterilization options as well. While effective, the use of chemical treatments in soil should be approached with caution, especially for indoor houseplants, due to potential toxicity. Always choose products that are safe for indoor use and follow the label instructions precisely. Chemical options include commercially available fungicides and pesticides.

A hydrogen peroxide solution can be another effective option. By mixing a solution of hydrogen peroxide with water (usually a 1:4 ratio of 3% hydrogen peroxide to water), and adding to your soil, the soil will be oxygenated which will kill off certain pathogens. Watering plants with a hydrogen peroxide solution can also help address overwatering issues by introducing oxygen.

There are also natural and biological methods to help you avoid introducing pests or disease through your soil. Beneficial microorganisms, such as mycorrhizae or other beneficial bacteria and fungi, can be added to help outcompete harmful pathogens and improve soil health. Mixing neem into the soil can also provide the plant with a natural fertilizer while simultaneously deterring soil-borne pests and diseases.

Regardless of the approach you choose to take to sanitize your soil, it's important that you also take bio security steps to avoid cross-contamination. Namely, use clean tools and containers when handling soil to prevent the spread of pests and diseases. Additionally, quarantine new plants to avoid introducing problems.

Preventing pest and disease issues in houseplants requires you to have an intentional approach to bio security that starts with healthy soil practices. By choosing the right treatment method when introducing new soil and maintaining good cultural practices when introducing new plants, houseplant entrepreneurs can ensure their plants remain healthy and vibrant, minimizing losses and maximizing customer satisfaction.

4 GROWING STRONG: THE RIGHT ENVIRONMENT AND TROUBLESHOOTING

Lily had an innate ability to nurture her houseplants. Her natural green thumb had intuitively guided her to optimize the temperature and humidity levels of her apartment to create an ideal environment for her plants. This careful calibration of her living space had turned her apartment into a thriving urban jungle. However, as her interest in expanding her botanical family grew, Lily recognized the necessity of creating specific microclimates to accommodate the diverse requirements of potential new additions.

Aware of the delicate balance required to maintain the health of various plant species, Lily contemplated options she might have to meet differing needs of plants, even within the same relatively small space. She could install a wire rack equipped with a small grow light; this would not only enhance the light available during the shorter days of winter but also could help her support the growth of plants that craved more light than her apartment could naturally offer. She also considered a strategy of rotating her plants to make the most of the natural light that was available at different times of the day. This approach would ensure that each plant received its fair share of sunlight but would require more work from her.

Lily also understood that expanding her plant collection would mean that she would need to thoroughly research the specific care requirements of each new type of plant she added. The one-size-fits-all approach that worked for her current collection wouldn't suffice in the long-term if she really wanted to expand. She would need to understand not just the humidity and light requirements of each new plant, but she'd also need to understand the optimal soil mixes that would best support the health and growth of new varieties. Even watering methods would need to be tailored to meet the distinct needs of certain types of plants. Ultimately, whether she could be successful nurturing a diverse range of houseplants would depend on her willingness to learn and adapt her care.

Managing Environmental Conditions

Once you've chosen the types of houseplants you will offer in your business, you'll need to ensure you're ready to provide them with the care they require. Houseplant health and growth are heavily influenced by the environment. This section will review how to create the perfect conditions for each species in your collection. Whether it's adjusting temperature, tweaking lighting, or managing humidity, you have options to mimic natural habitats and keep your plants thriving.

<u>Temperature</u>

Most houseplants thrive in temperatures between 60-75°F (15-24°C). Your environment might already achieve this general range. Also consider that there may be microenvironments within your larger space where the temperature could be cooler or warmer than the rest of the room, and this could affect the wellbeing of plants in that space. As a general rule, avoid placing plants near drafts or heat sources. As your business grows, you may want to use programmable thermostats to help maintain stable temperatures.

In some cases, you may need to consider investing in a good heating or cooling system. This can be an expensive upfront cost; it's important to also consider the long-term operating costs of any heating or cooling system, in addition to the upfront cost. By choosing energy-efficient models you can reduce your long-term costs and set yourself up for better results. Additionally, steps like insulation and having energy-efficient windows can help maintain stable temperatures and reduce energy bills.

Lighting

Understanding the light requirements of each plant type you will maintain is critically important. You'll need to know whether each type of plant you have requires low light, indirect light or will only thrive with direct sunlight. Understanding this can help you position plants within your space. Positioning plants, or even rotating plants to make the most of your available natural light can help minimize the need to add artificial lighting.

Using grow lights for plants that need more light than your space naturally provides is also an option, though there are cost implications. If you feel grow lights are required for your business to succeed, LED grow lights are more energy-efficient and have a longer lifespan than fluorescent bulbs, which can reduce your electricity costs and replacement frequency.

Humidity

Tropical plants, in particular, require higher humidity levels. You can add humidity to your natural environment by using room humidifiers, misting plants regularly, or even simply placing plants on a tray of water and pebbles to increase the humidity around them.

Although humidifiers do consume electricity, you can minimize costs by using them only during dry months or in specific hours of the day. Misting and pebble trays are low-cost options, but the downside is that they require more consistent effort.

Practical Advice for Managing Costs

In general, if your environment requires that you artificially adjust the temperature, lighting or humidity, do your research and assess the cost and energy consumption of any appliances or types of bulbs you might see.

Using timers for lights and thermostats can help you more efficiently manage your energy use, ensuring that you only use what you need. Grouping plants with similar environmental needs together to allow you to maintain targeted microclimates is another practical tip to help you reduce the need to alter the conditions of an entire space.

By using digital thermometers and hygrometers, you can monitor your environmental conditions closely. This can help you optimize the environmental conditions by identifying potential problems before they become too extreme, helping to ensure plant health.

Consider too, whether you have an opportunity to incorporate sustainable practices to help you reduce costs and operate an environmentally friendly business. Steps like collecting rainwater for irrigation can reduce water bills. Similarly, using natural light as much as possible can reduce or eliminate the need for artificial lighting. You can also take simple steps like providing your houseplants with good air circulation by opening windows to help manage both temperature and humidity levels efficiently.

If you do need to buy equipment to maintain the appropriate environment, do your research to help manage costs. Look for sales, used items or wholesale options for grow lights, humidifiers, and thermostats. Calculate the cost of creating the ideal environment against the potential return. Rare or high-demand plants that fetch a higher price may justify higher upfront costs for precise environmental control.

Balancing the environmental needs of plants with the operational costs of running a houseplant business requires careful planning and optimization. By using sustainable low or no cost options wherever possible, investing in energy efficient systems, monitoring conditions closely, and adopting cost-saving measures, you can create a thriving environment for your plants and a profitable business model.

Soil Mixes and Growing Mediums

Making the right choice about the soil mix or growing medium you'll use sets the stage for your houseplants' future. The perfect mix should be like a gourmet meal for your plants—packed with nutrients and consisting of well-draining material and just the right texture. Whether you're looking for soilless mixes for an orchid or hunting down the perfect pH balance for your ferns, understanding what makes each plant tick is key.

If you're thinking of shipping your plants, the weight of your growing medium can be a game-changer, either driving up or helping you manage shipping costs. Lighter can be kinder to your wallet, but some of your bigger leafy friends might need the heft of a denser soil mixture to stay in place.

Let's talk about the nitty-gritty—drainage and aeration are critical to plant health. Nobody likes soggy feet, especially plants. Mixing in some perlite, vermiculite, or sand can help keep the air flowing and roots happy. But remember, with plants, everything is a balancing act! Too soggy is bad and too dry isn't good either. Peat moss and coco coir can be your friends for keeping a potting mix just moist enough.

Nutrition is important too. Healthy soil equals happy plants. Mixing in some compost or well-rotted manure can give your plants a buffet of nutrients. And if you're playing the long game, some slow-release fertilizer can keep them munching happily for months.

pH levels are like the secret sauce of nutrient uptake. Most houseplants thrive on a slightly acidic to neutral pH (around 6.0-7.0). A quick pH test can save you from a lot of head-scratching later. And when it comes to soil structure, think of it as the plant's personal fitness trainer—it shapes those roots and helps them slurp up water and absorb nutrients efficiently.

Starting with a commercial potting mix can be a good initial choice, but as you get to know your plants, you might want to mix your own special blend tailored to their needs. And here's a factor to consider: going organic can not only boost your plants but can also appeal to eco-conscious customers. Just keep in mind, organic might need more TLC in terms of nutrient maintenance.

So, there you have it! Choosing the right soil is a big step towards a thriving plant business. Keep experimenting, keep learning, and your plants (and customers) will thank you.

Fertilizers and Nutrient Requirements

Well-fed plants are happy plants! Getting the lowdown on what each of your plants craves in terms of nutrients will be important to help you select the right nutrient mix and schedule. Even the best soil blend will require some level of ongoing nutrient monitoring and supplements.

<u>Nutrition and Soil Health: The Basics</u>

Plants just don't subscribe to the "eat whatever, whenever" lifestyle. They have specific dietary needs that change at different times over the course of their lives. They need more during phases of active growing than they do when they're kicking back and relaxing in dormancy.

This is where fertilizer comes into play, enabling you to provide a personalized menu for your plants. Whether you're going organic or synthetic, understanding and paying attention to the N-P-K (Nitrogen-Phosphorus-Potassium) ratios on fertilizer labels is like choosing the right dish for a healthy dinner. These nutrients are the main course for plant growth, each bringing something special to the table:

- Nitrogen (N) jazzes up leaf and stem growth, keeping things green and lush.

- Phosphorus (P) is all about the roots, flowers, seeds, and fruits—think of it as the plant's development booster.

- Potassium (K) is the health guru, aiding in water uptake, enzyme action, and disease resistance.

You'll be playing the role of matchmaker when choosing the perfect fertilizer. You've got to know your plant's profile—what stage of life it's in, what it's lacking, and what it's got extra of, and find a fertilizer to bring it as close as possible to its natural, perfect state. A soil test will be your best friend here, revealing what's under the surface and helping you pick the right supplement.

Fertilizer 101: Picking Your Potion

While knowing your current soil state, and your plant's unique needs is crucial, there are some general guidelines to learn. Young plants or fresh transplants tend to love a high-phosphorus mix, which encourages them to put down roots in their new home. Established green plants tend to prefer a more balanced diet or something that boosts their special attribute, be it leafy growth or blooming beautiful flowers.

When it comes to applying fertilizer, you have many different options. Liquid fertilizers offer a quick fix and can be great to help balance an immediate problem. Granular fertilizers are ideal for a longer-term, balanced management approach and provide a slow-release energy supply. And of course, there are organic options for the eco-conscious. Just remember, more is not always better. Stick to the feeding schedule on the label and avoid overindulging your plants.

Seasonal Feeding Frenzies

Plants' needs change over time, they tend to have their seasons of both feast and fast. Spring and summer are generally focused on growth, meaning your plants will tend to be hungrier for nutrients during these times. Come fall and winter, it's time to dial it back and let them rest.

In the end, getting your plants' nutrition right is about playing detective, matchmaker, chef, and sometimes personal trainer. When in doubt, start with a balanced fertilizer, watch how your green friend responds, and adjust your fertilizing schedule and formula as you go. Remember, every plant has its quirks, so tailor your care to each green buddy for the best results. Keep notes, stay curious, and before you know it, you'll have a thriving plant family.

Water Management

You're going to need to think about water too! Not all water is created equal, especially when it comes to our green friends. Tap water can be a cocktail of chlorine and fluoride, which can be big problems for plants. In terms of water quantity, houseplants require water, but not too much and not too little. Gaining an understanding of how water quality, water quantity and watering techniques affect plant health will help you be successful.

How Water Quality Affects Plants

Tap water often contains high levels of chlorine and fluoride that can be harmful. Excessive fluoride can accumulate in the soil, which may affect the plant's ability to absorb nutrients. This can lead to nutrient deficiencies and other health issues. Chlorine can cause leaf burn and inhibit root growth when it accumulates in high concentrations in a plant's tissues.

Using distilled water or filtered water for houseplants can help you avoid potential problems associated with fluoridated water and excessive chlorine. While it's possible to purchase distilled or filtered water for your plants, as you add additional plants the cost and inconvenience of buying and moving gallons of store-bought water can quickly become a financial and logistical nightmare. A great option if you live in an area with fluoridated water is to invest in a reverse osmosis (RO) filtration system.

An RO system can significantly improve the quality of water. RO systems use a multi-stage filtration process and are highly effective at removing a wide range of contaminants, including chlorine and fluoride, as well as salts, bacteria, and heavy metals, which can also be harmful to plant health. RO systems produce consistent, high-quality water and help you prevent potential toxicity problems from impacting your plants. Plants watered with RO water will generally grow better and in a healthier way since the water is free from contaminants that can interfere with nutrient uptake and overall plant health. It's important to be aware, however, that RO water is stripped of most minerals, including minerals that are beneficial for plants. You may need to supplement RO water with specific minerals or fertilizers that the plant would otherwise obtain from natural water sources.

The initial setup cost and ongoing maintenance of RO systems can be a factor. However, for serious horticulturists, the investment is typically well justified by the superior water quality and resulting plant health benefits.

If your water supply comes from a well, it might naturally offer a reliable and healthy water source for your plants without requiring filtration, but this is not always the case. Well water is generally free of additives like fluoride, but it's important to have your well water tested and to understand the potential drawbacks or considerations of using your specific well water to water your houseplants.

Well water can have a high mineral content, which could lead to a buildup of salts and minerals in your plants' soil over time. The mineral content of some well water can impact the pH level of a plant's soil; this can affect the plant's ability to absorb nutrients. Well water can potentially also contain contaminants such as bacteria, pesticides, or heavy metals, especially if the well is located near agricultural or industrial areas. These contaminants can be harmful to plants and may also affect human health.

Additionally, well water can be hard, meaning it contains high levels of calcium and magnesium. While these minerals are not harmful to plants, they can contribute to the buildup of scale in pots and soil and may require additional maintenance over time to prevent issues.

To mitigate these potential drawbacks, have your well water tested regularly for contaminants and mineral content. If necessary, consider using a water softener or filtration system to help improve the quality of your water for your plants.

Finally, collecting and using rainwater, if you are able to do so, can be a great alternative to tap water. Rainwater is naturally soft water and it's also free of additives; this makes it ideal for watering plants. This is also an environmentally friendly option, and if you are able to water your plants with rainwater this could become part of your business's brand story and could help you appeal to an environmentally conscious customer base.

Watering Techniques

Plants can be so picky! A plant that is not watered will die, and overwatering is also a common cause of plant death. There are techniques such as bottom watering that can encourage healthy root growth for certain plants and minimize the risk of overwatering. Or perhaps, investing in a drip irrigation system or misting system would be more appropriate for your plants and circumstances. There are different levels of sophistication and investment required depending on the watering approach you choose. It is possible to start at a small scale, with a manual approach and be successful and then upgrade your watering system in the future.

Bottom Watering

Bottom watering is a low-tech watering technique that is super helpful for a houseplant entrepreneur to know. Water is absorbed from the bottom of the pot upward into the soil, rather than pouring water over the top of the soil. This method encourages the plant roots to grow downward as they seek moisture, which for many plant types can lead to a stronger root system. This can be a particularly beneficial watering technique for plants that are sensitive to moisture on their leaves, or that are prone to disease caused by overwatering.

If you are raising plants that could benefit from bottom

watering, it's an easy technique to deploy. Simply start with a container that is larger and deeper than the plant's pot and ensure the container can hold water. Importantly, the plant pot must also have drainage holes at the bottom. Add water to the larger container; the level of water should be enough to reach the bottom part of the plant pot, but not so high that it goes over the top edge of the pot. Place the plant pot in the outer container. The process of capillary action will move the water up through the drainage holes in the plant's pot and moisten the soil from the bottom up. Let the plant sit in this outer watering container until the topsoil feels moist to the touch. This can take anywhere from 10 minutes to an hour, depending on the size of the pot and the dryness of the soil. Once the soil is moist, remove the pot from the water and let it drain thoroughly to help prevent any excess water from causing root rot.

Bottom watering houseplants can help prevent overwatering. The soil absorbs water up to a point of saturation and you're not adding water to the surface. This can also minimize foliage disease; by keeping water off the plant's leaves, you reduce the risk of common fungal diseases that thrive in moist conditions. This method can also be a way to efficiently manage water consumption, as it reduces evaporation and ensures that water goes directly to where the plant needs it most—at the roots. Conversely, plants that only receive watering through regular top watering can experience salt buildup on the soil surface. Bottom watering helps distribute salts more evenly or push them deeper into the soil and away from the root zone.

But bottom watering is not suitable for all plants. Some plants prefer dry conditions or have shallow root systems and may not get what they need from bottom watering. Like any watering technique, monitoring is key. It's important to check the soil to ensure it is adequately moistened, as some compacted soils or pots with insufficient drainage may not effectively wick up water. If you do choose to experiment with bottom watering, occasionally, it can be beneficial to water from the top to further flush out any salt buildup in the soil, this can also help ensure the soil is evenly moistened and aerated.

Drip Irrigation

Adding a drip irrigation system when starting a houseplant side hustle can be a time saving option that reduces demand on your time. Drip irrigation systems offer many benefits over manual watering and can become especially appealing as your business grows.

Drip irrigation watering systems deliver water that is targeted directly to the base of each plant, reducing waste, and ensuring that water goes exactly where it's needed. Since water is delivered near the soil surface and directly to the root zone, less water is lost to evaporation compared to surface watering or misting. Drip systems help conserve water by using it more efficiently, which makes drip irrigation an eco-friendly and cost-effective option, especially in areas with water use restrictions or high water costs.

Once set up, a drip irrigation system can be automated with timers, which can free up significant amounts of time that would otherwise be spent hand-watering, while also delivering a consistent watering experience to plants. These systems provide consistent moisture levels which is crucial for plant health and growth; moisture levels can be maintained without the need to remember to water or worrying about over- or under-watering. Consistent and accurate water delivery can lead to more uniform plant growth and potentially higher yields for plants that are grown for their fruit or flowers.

Another benefit of drip irrigation systems is that they can reduce the risk of certain types of plant disease. By minimizing water contact with leaves, drip irrigation can lower the humidity around plants, reducing the risk of fungal diseases.

Integrating a drip irrigation system into a houseplant side hustle can significantly enhance your operational efficiency, plant health, and profitability, making it a worthwhile consideration for entrepreneurs looking to scale their operations while maintaining or improving plant care standards. While the benefits are significant, it's important to consider the initial cost and the need for regular maintenance to prevent clogs and leaks when evaluating whether a drip irrigation system is right for you. You can also expect a learning curve associated with setting up and optimizing the system. For very small operations or those with a highly diverse range of plants, the flexibility of hand-watering might initially be a better choice.

Misting Systems

Misting systems, or even manual misting with a spray bottle can be a real benefit to certain types of houseplants, particularly those that thrive in high humidity environments. Plants like ferns, orchids, air plants and tropical plants which originate from humid rainforest climates can struggle in the dry air of heated or air-conditioned homes. If you plan to raise these types of plants, it's important to adjust their environment to mimic their natural conditions as closely as possible. For some plants, a misting system can help accomplish this and is another watering system to consider in certain circumstances.

Misting systems can vary in terms of their level of sophistication, from complex automated setups to simple manual spray bottles. Automated systems typically consist of a series of nozzles that are connected to a water source and a timer, which periodically releases a fine spray of water into the air, mimicking the humid conditions of a plant's natural habitat. The increased moisture in the air helps the plants absorb water through their leaves, which is particularly beneficial for plants that have a lot of leaf surface area, and plants that are adapted to absorb moisture from the air.

Misting systems are an effective way to increase the local humidity level around plants, which can benefit some plants and is essential for tropical varieties. By simulating a plant's natural environment, misting can improve growth, leaf texture, and overall plant health. Misting is also great for keeping plant leaves clean and free from dust, which not only keeps them pretty, but allows for better photosynthesis and respiration, and can contribute to a healthier plant.

For large collections of tropical plants or commercial operations, automated misting systems can save considerable time and effort by providing consistent humidity with minimal daily manual work. A major downside, however, is that overuse of misting systems can contribute to disease, with too much moisture on leaves promoting fungal diseases and leaf rot. It's not the right approach for all types of plants.

Automated misting systems require regular maintenance to prevent clogs in the nozzles and ensure the system operates effectively. Setting up an automated misting system does involve an initial investment and ongoing costs for water and electricity use.

While automated misting systems can provide consistent humidity that is necessary for certain houseplants on a larger scale, a humidifier or even a simple spray bottle can offer cost-effective solutions for small-scale operations. Spray bottles allow for targeted, controlled misting, making them an ideal low-tech choice for houseplant entrepreneurs starting with a limited budget or those who prefer a more hands-on approach to plant care.

Consider the types of plants you plan to raise, their preferred conditions and natural environment. Understand your options to determine the approach that best balances your plants' needs, your capacity for manual watering work and your budget.

Monitoring Moisture

Regardless of the watering method or methods that you choose—whether bottom watering, drip irrigation, mister systems, spray bottles, or manual top watering—it is important that you monitor the moisture levels of your plants and soil closely and adjust your watering process as needed. Be vigilant in your efforts to ensure your plants receive just the right amount of water, and that the level of water they receive and the method they receive it from reflects their natural habitat conditions. This will promote optimal health and growth.

A simple, low-tech technique to monitor the moisture level of your plants is to feel the soil. Insert your finger into the soil up to your second knuckle. If the soil feels dry at this depth, it's probably time to water. For smaller pots, a quick lift can indicate how wet the soil is based on the plant and pot's weight.

For a more precise measurement, a moisture meter can become a valuable tool. Inserted into the soil, a moisture meter will give you an instant reading of the moisture level. This tool is particularly useful for larger pots or for plants that require you to maintain a very specific moisture levels.

Always observe the signs your plant gives you. Plants often show visible signs when they need water. Wilting, drooping leaves, or soil pulling away from a pot's edge can all indicate under-watering. Yellowing leaves or edema (blisters on the leaves) may indicate over-watering.

If you are bottom watering or using a drip irrigation system, look to your drainage tray. The amount of water that remains in the tray after a few hours can indicate how much water the soil is absorbing. Excess water should be emptied to prevent root rot, and for future waterings you can scale back the amount of water you add.

While the frequency of your monitoring practices will depend on the plant type, environmental conditions, and the season, establishing a regular routine is key. Most houseplants benefit from a check every 1-2 days. Plants typically require more frequent watering during their growing season (spring and summer) and less during dormant periods (fall and winter). Monitor this and adjust your watering accordingly.

If you do find that your plants are consistently either too dry or too wet, adjust the amount of water you give at each watering. For drip systems, this may mean adjusting the timer or emitter output. Sometimes, it's not about how much water you give but how often. Some plants prefer a thorough soaking less frequently, while others benefit from smaller, more frequent waterings. If certain plants are not thriving with your current method of watering, consider changing it. You can also try adjusting the light, humidity, and temperature which can all affect how quickly soil dries out. Adding a layer of mulch or moss to the soil surface can also help retain moisture in the soil, reducing the need for frequent waterings.

Be prepared to adjust your watering routine in response to environmental factors and what you observe during routine monitoring. Documenting your watering schedule, methods, and plant responses can help you fine-tune your approach over time. Different plants have vastly different watering needs; educate yourself on the needs of your plants. Successful houseplant care revolves around attentiveness and adaptability to each plant's needs. By monitoring soil moisture and adjusting watering practices, you can ensure the health of your houseplants and enhance the ultimate success of your houseplant business.

Troubleshooting Common Plant Health Issues

No matter how diligent you are, the world of houseplant care will not always be smooth sailing. You'll find that each plant type brings its own set of challenges. Over time, you'll become a true plant whisperer, able to tackle these hurdles head-on. Let's dive into some common houseplant challenges you might encounter.

<u>The Case of the Yellowing Leaves</u>

If you find that a once thriving plant is suddenly sporting some less-than-fashionable yellow leaves, it's time to go into detective mode. In many cases, yellow leaves can be a sign of overwatering. Check the plant's soil and, if you find that it's soggier than a marsh, it's time to adjust your watering schedule and make sure the soil has time to dry out between waterings. This should help your plant's leaves return to a healthier green hue.

<u>The Mystery of the Leggy Plant</u>

What about a mature plant that looks more like a lanky teenager than a full-bodied plant? The likely culprit in this case is not enough light! Plants that are exhibiting weak, but long growth are stretching towards the light and are investing their resources in growing in height rather than in growth quality. A quick rearrangement of your plant setup is usually the answer. When your plant is receiving its needed daily dose of sunshine, you'll find that the growth pattern should change, and over time your plant will once again be compact and happy.

The Puzzle of the Pests

If you find yourself hosting an unwelcome pest party with aphids or mealybugs crashing the scene, stay calm. Instead of reaching for harsh chemicals, start by wiping down the plants' leaves with a neem oil solution, a natural pest deterrent. Pest challenges can require more than an initial neem oil treatment, but neem oil is nearly always a safe place to start. You should take steps to learn how to fully address and prevent such problems as you encounter them. Consult with a local nursery or try taking close-up pictures of your plant's problem area and sharing them in an online plant community if you need some expert advice diagnosing and addressing a specific pest issue.

A World of Resources

You'll find yourself periodically in this detective role trying to understand and adjust the conditions for a plant that is struggling. Healthy plants begin with proactive plant care. Keeping your leafy friends happy often means more than just occasional water and light. You'll need to create a nurturing environment, complete with the right nutrients, watering patterns, and a loving touch. By understanding and providing your plants with the care requirements specific to their needs, you'll avoid many common challenges. And by keeping diligent, careful watch over your plants, you'll be able to spot and address problems early.

There is a world of plant literature available to help you expand your knowledge. The couple common plant challenges addressed in this book are far from a comprehensive list of the challenges you'll encounter. It's wise to invest in a couple reliable, go-to guides to have on your shelf. "The New Plant Parent" by

Darryl Cheng and "How Not to Kill Your Houseplant" by Veronica Peerless are just a couple such resources to consider. You'll find that books such as these will offer in-depth solutions to common problems and also will deepen your understanding of plant care, getting you ready to tackle any challenge that might come your way.

5 CUTTINGS TO CASH: PROPAGATING YOUR WAY TO PROFIT

Lily already had some level of plant propagation experience, having taken cuttings and planted certain types of seeds. She had also occasionally separated and started offsets from her spider plant. But she didn't want her business to be limited by only what she already knew about plant reproduction. Her curiosity and ambition pushed her into a whirl of research aiming to expand her repertoire of propagation methods.

As she pored over gardening books and clicked her way through online forums, Lily noted the various propagation techniques that were suited to different types of plants. She understood that while taking cuttings and starting seeds were common methods, each type of plant had its unique requirements and preferred methods of propagation.

Division, in particular, intrigued her as it involved separating a larger plant into smaller, individually viable sections, a method especially effective for her bushier, root-bound plants. She also was intrigued by the more sophisticated technique of air layering, a method that fascinated her with its ability to generate roots directly on the branches of a plant while still attached to the parent. This promised a new level of complexity and challenge, and Lily was eager to give it a try. She also ventured into learning about spore propagation, a method that is less commonly applied in casual horticulture but prevalent for those who raise ferns and mosses. Her research opened a new dimension in her gardening practice, offering insights into the vast diversity of plant life and new plant reproduction techniques for her to understand.

Plan Propagation

To be successful at raising houseplants, it's necessary to understand the fundamentals of plant reproduction. Whether it's seeds, cuttings, divisions, layering or something more exotic and specialized, the propagation method you choose is like picking the right tool for the job. Knowing your plants inside and out is key. Not all plants like to reproduce the same way. Some might prefer a simple snip and dip in water, while others might need a bit more TLC with seeds or a cozy blanket of soil through layering. A high-level understanding of common propagation methods, coupled with additional research specific to the plants you plan to raise, will help you pick the propagation method that will work best for you.

Start with a Healthy Parent Plant

A healthy parent plant is a crucial requirement of effective houseplant propagation. Using a sick or young plant could lead to failed propagation or even an illness spreading. Before propagating a plant, evaluate its health.

Keep an eye out for symptoms such as weak, spindly, or lanky growth, which can indicate insufficient light or other unfavorable growing circumstances. This can impact the quality and vigor of cuttings or seeds. Examine the parent plant's leaves for any yellowing, browning, or other discolorations, which might point to a disease, nutrient shortage, or environmental stressors.

Additionally, check the parent plant for pests like mealybugs, scale, aphids, or mites. Pests can easily spread from infected plants to their offspring, causing even more problems. During the propagation process, pathogens can actually survive in a plant's tissues and spread to the cuttings or seeds. Treat any infestations of pests right away.

Other indicators that point to a problem with the parent plant include wilting, leaf spots, mold, or other odd developments. A parent plant might not be mature enough to produce healthy cuttings or seeds if its growth is slowed down or inhibited. Plants that are too young lack the reserves of energy required to sustain the growth of new plants. Plants that are root-bound are also inappropriate candidates for propagation, as they may not be able to recuperate from the stress and their offspring may not root well.

A lack of energy, liveliness, and general health concerns are another clear sign of a sick parent plant. Selecting healthy, disease-free, and rapidly growing parent plants is crucial when propagating new plants. You will increase your success rate as a houseplant entrepreneur by starting with only healthy, mature parent plants. Once you have healthy parent plants, selecting the propagation method suited to that type of plant is your next task. There are multiple methods, each appropriate for certain types of plants and circumstances.

Seed Starting

Starting new plants from seeds is perhaps the most traditional form of plant propagation. Germinating seeds usually takes longer than other propagation methods and produces more genetic variability in plant offspring.

Seed starting allows gardeners to raise large numbers of plants and can be rewarding. Picture it: tiny seeds blossoming into lush, vibrant plants all thanks to your care. It's like being present at the birth of your plant babies—a bit magical. Starting plants from seeds can be a great option for expanding your indoor jungle or adding some exclusive, home-grown hybrids to your plant side hustle.

Let's break down this seed-sprouting journey, step by step. First things first, you'll need some seeds. Pick your plant contenders—maybe some herbs to spice up the kitchen, or how about some stunning flowers to dazzle a living space? Once you've got your seeds, grab some seed starting mix. This stuff is like a cozy blanket for your seeds, providing them with the perfect spot to germinate and grow.

Fill some small pots or seed trays with your starting mix, gently press the seeds into the soil (check the seed packet to understand how deep they like to be planted) and cover them up with a sprinkle of soil. Give them a good drink with a gentle shower from a spray bottle—you're aiming for moist soil, not a mudslide. Pop those pots in a warm spot with plenty of indirect light.

From there, patience is key. Keep the soil moist with your trusty spray bottle and wait for the magic to happen. When those green shoots start to show their faces, it's like your plant babies are waving hello to the world. If you're planting a variety of seeds, be sure to take time to label your pots.

Once your seedlings have grown up a bit and look strong enough to handle the real world (aka your living room, balcony, or garden), it's time to introduce them to their new pots. Be gentle—they're still young; transplant them carefully.

Seed starting isn't just planting; it's creating life from the tiniest of beginnings. It's perfect for those looking to grow their plant collection, start a side hustle with unique offerings, or simply those who enjoy the thrill of watching life unfold.

There are many types of houseplants that are able to reproduce through seeds. The resulting plants won't be genetically identical to the parent plant – which can be a good or bad thing, depending on your goals. If you're going for genetic variation or attempting to crossbreed plants, this is the method to turn to.

Taking Cuttings

Propagating plants through cuttings is like giving your plants a fresh start, and it's a fantastic way to stock up a plant side hustle with young, new plants. Let's break down this super simple yet oh-so-rewarding process, shall we?

You snip a piece off your plant, stick it in some soil or water, and watch as it grows roots and becomes a brand-new plant. It's like magic, but with more chlorophyll. The superstar plants who thrive with this method include the ever-popular Pothos, the lovely Philodendron, and the vibrant Tradescantia. These plants are so eager to root, you'll feel like a green-thumbed wizard in no time at all.

To make this magic happen, grab a clean, sharp pair of scissors or a knife. Look for a healthy, happy stem with at least a couple of leaves on it, and snip just below a leaf node (that's the little bump where leaves grow out of the stem). From there you have options. One path is to pop your cutting into a glass jar filled with water. Make sure those leaf nodes are submerged, while keeping the actual leaves high and dry. Alternatively, you can place your cuttings in soil instead of water, dip the end of the cutting in some rooting hormone (not totally necessary, but it definitely speeds up the process and increases your odds of success) and stick it into moist potting mix. Whether you choose water or soil, give your new cuttings plenty of indirect light and keep them nice and warm.

This is when the waiting game begins. Keep an eye on your water level if you're going the aquatic route and change it every few days to keep things fresh. For soil, keep the mix lightly moist but not soggy. In a few weeks, you should see roots starting to venture out. Most cuttings thrive when misted with water once or twice a day; this helps the young plant maintain humidity. When they're a couple of inches long, it's time to pot those water babies into soil. For soil-grown cuttings, once they're rooted and robust, they're ready to start their new life as a potted plant. You can try gently pulling the cutting upwards to assess whether it's firmly planted in the soil and holding its own with new roots.

Environmental conditions can impact the amount of time it takes for a cutting to establish roots. Cuttings generally require a warm and stable temperature to promote the formation of roots. Warmer temperatures encourage root growth, while cooler temperatures can slow down the process. For most plants, temperatures between 65-75F (18-24C) are ideal for root development. In terms of humidity, higher humidity levels can help prevent excessive moisture loss from the cutting and can create a favorable environment for root initiation. In drier conditions, the cutting may struggle to retain sufficient moisture, which can hinder root development. Direct sunlight is generally not recommended for newly rooted cuttings, but providing adequate indirect light does help support the development of roots and new growth. Insufficient light can slow down the rooting process, while excessive light can lead to stress and dehydration.

Proper air circulation will help prevent fungal diseases in your cuttings and promote healthy root development. Stagnant air can lead to excess moisture around the cutting, increasing the risk of rot, while excessive airflow may cause the cutting to dry out too quickly.

Providing appropriate rooting hormones and essential nutrients can also influence the speed and success of root development in cuttings. Gardeners often choose to dip the cut end of the stem into a rooting hormone powder, gel, or liquid before planting it in soil or adding to water. Rooting hormones are substances that stimulate root growth in plant cuttings, enhancing the chances of successful root development and, ultimately, the survival and growth of new plants. These hormones can be synthetic or natural and are primarily used to encourage cuttings to develop strong, healthy roots more quickly than they might on their own. Applying rooting hormone to the cut end of your cuttings will help you accelerate root formation, increase the uniformity of the roots that develop and will enhance the overall success rate of your propagation process.

Overall, cuttings offer a low-cost way to expand your plant collection and share your favorites with friends or customers. This is a faster process than starting from seed, and the plants you produce will always be genetic clones to the parent plant. Unlike seeds, propagating by taking cuttings ensures genetic uniformity, which gives you highly predictable results. This ensures that the new plant will have the same characteristics, such as leaf shape, flower color, and growth habit, as the original plant. This makes it easy for a houseplant seller to accurately describe the plant that their buyers are purchasing, even before it reaches maturity.

Assessing if a Plant can Tolerate Cuttings

To understand whether your houseplant can tolerate you taking cuttings, research the specific type of plant and assess its overall health. Consider the growth rate of the plant. Some houseplants are prolific growers and can readily produce new growth even after multiple recent cuttings. Be mindful not to overdo it; excessive cutting can still stress a plant. Some plants are known for their ability to readily root from cuttings, while others may be more sensitive to this propagation method. Again, research the specific characteristics of your plant to understand its typical response to propagation, and whether this method makes sense.

Also consider the time of year and the stage of growth your plant is in. Plants are often more resilient to the stress of cuttings during their active growing season, when they are naturally producing new growth.

If your plant tolerates regular pruning without significant negative effects on its overall health and growth, it will probably also be more likely to tolerate the process of taking cuttings. Pay attention to how the plant responds to pruning or cutting. If the plant quickly rebounds and continues to grow vigorously, it may indicate it's a great candidate for the process.

When to Take Cuttings for Sale

If you plan to sell cuttings online, it's important to allow the cutting to establish roots before sending. This will help ensure the cuttings survive transit. The length of time to wait between taking a cutting and shipping depends heavily on the specific plant type and the rooting method used, though there are some general guidelines to help you make this decision.

If you are rooting the cutting in water, you should wait to ship until the roots are at least a few inches long and are well-established. This could take several weeks, depending on the plant type. For cuttings rooted in soil or a similar growing medium, it's advisable to wait until the roots have developed a healthy root system and the cutting shows signs of new growth. This process generally takes between 4 and 6 weeks.

When shipping rooted cuttings, take special care when packing them to protect their delicate young roots and foliage during transit.

Divisions

Propagating through division allows you to create two (or more) plants from one. It's a fairly straightforward concept and doesn't require much more than your hands and a sharp knife. This method works wonders for houseplants that grow in clumps or that have multiple stems that emerge separately from the soil. It's an ideal way to multiply your plant collection or stock up inventory.

Spring or early summer are typically the ideal times of year to consider dividing larger plants. Some houseplants practically beg for division, making them perfect candidates for this propagation technique. These include Peace Lilies, Spider Plants, and Snake Plants. Without division, over time these plants can get crowded in their pots; dividing them not only gives you more plants to sell but also helps keep your original plant healthy and happy.

To divide a plant, gently remove it from its pot and shake off excess soil to reveal the roots. Look for natural separations or clumps. Using your hands or a clean, sharp knife, gently divide the plant into smaller sections, making sure each section has a good chunk of roots attached. Repot each new plant into fresh soil, water them well, and voilà—you've got new plants to nurture or sell!

Layering

Layering is another propagation technique that is appropriate for certain types of plants. Again, it's an easy to learn process that feels a bit like a fun science experiment. When propagating through layering you are essentially coaxing a part of the plant to grow new roots while it's still attached to the mother plant. The new plantlet draws water and nutrients from the parent until it's strong enough to fend for itself.

Layering requires just a few simple tools that you probably have lying around: a sharp knife, some toothpicks, and a bit of soil or sphagnum moss.

Layering can work well for propagating plants that have long, flexible stems or vines—think Pothos, Philodendrons, and certain types of Ivy. Plants whose stems can easily be bent down to the soil or moss without breaking are potential layering candidates.

Simply choose a healthy stem and make a small cut or notch just below a leaf node (that's where the roots tend to sprout). If you want, you can prop the cut open with a toothpick. Then, pin this part down into a pot filled with soil or wrap it in moist sphagnum moss, securing it with twine or a bobby pin. Keep it moist, and in a few weeks, you should see roots begin to form. Once the roots are hearty enough, you can cut the new plantlet from the mother plant and plant it in its very own pot.

Layering is a gentle, nurturing way to propagate, and it's super satisfying to watch those new roots take hold, knowing you helped make it happen. Patience is key. Nature can't be rushed, but the reward of new plant life is well worth the wait.

<u>Air Layering</u>

Air layering is a variation on layering that works well for woody plants or those with thicker stems that don't take well to simpler propagation methods. A couple common contenders for air layering are Monsteras, Rubber Trees, and Fiddle Leaf Figs. Like layering, the idea is to encourage a stem to root while it's still attached and happily growing on the parent plant.

Choose a healthy stem and make a small upward slit or remove a ring of bark, exposing the inner layer. This spot is where you'll coax those roots to emerge from. Moisten some sphagnum moss and wrap it around the wounded area, then snugly cover it with plastic wrap to keep moisture in. Secure everything with tape, string, or twist ties – whatever keeps it tight and tidy. The moss acts like a cozy little nursery for new roots to develop right on the stem. Keep an eye on the moisture level, and after a few weeks or months (patience, my friends!), you should see roots poking through. Once you've got a good root ball, you can cut the stem below the roots and pot up your brand-new plant!

Air layering is a fantastic way to get larger, more established plants right from the get-go. It's a fun experiment with a pretty high success rate, making it a great propagation technique to become familiar with.

Offsets or Pups

Ever notice those cute little baby plants, aka offsets or pups, that your houseplants start popping out when they're feeling extra happy and loved? Well, it turns out these little guys are your ticket to easily multiplying your plant family. Offsets are basically mini-me's of your plants that grow from the base or the sides of the mother plant. They're like nature's little bonuses, giving you brand new plants without much fuss.

Some of the champion producers of offsets include the beloved Snake Plant, the ever-so-charming Spider Plant, and certain plump succulents like Echeverias and Haworthias.

Here's how to work this magic: Once you spot a pup that has a few leaves of its own and looks sturdy enough to venture out into the world (usually a couple of inches tall), it's go time. With a clean, sharp knife or pair of scissors, gently separate the offset from the mother plant, making sure to get a good chunk of roots if they've developed. No roots yet? No need to panic! Some pups can start rootless and still grow up to be strong, independent plants.

Next up, pot your new baby plant in a cozy pot with well-draining soil, give it a warm welcome with a little water, and voila! You've got yourself a new plant pal. Keep the soil slightly moist and place your pup in a warm, bright spot with indirect light, to give it all the encouragement it needs to flourish.

6 THE GARDENER'S TOOLKIT: ESSENTIALS FOR A FLOURISHING SIDE HUSTLE

For Lily, embarking on her houseplant side hustle hadn't required a significant upfront investment in supplies. Her strategy was simple — leverage the lush collection of houseplants she already nurtured in her home. By taking cuttings from these thriving plants, she utilized the resources at her fingertips to create new life and potential profit. The initial outlay was minimal: a few extra pots to house her propagating plants, a basic plastic seed tray with a dome to maintain optimal humidity for her tender seedlings, and a new water bottle for misting to provide her plants the gentle moisture they needed.

On the business side, Lily embraced a practical and sustainable approach. She initially repurposed packing materials for shipping her plants, reflecting her commitment to both cost-efficiency and environmental responsibility. To keep her burgeoning business organized, a couple of notebooks became her command center, holding her business task lists, tracking her inventory, and jotting down ideas for future growth. This low-barrier entry into the houseplant market allowed Lily to focus on what she loved — growing and sharing her plants — while slowly building a foundation for a sustainable side hustle rooted in her passion and resourcefulness.

Equipment and Supplies

In addition to selecting plants and understanding how to propagate them, you will also need some basic equipment and supplies to get a houseplant side hustle started. Remember, starting a houseplant side hustle doesn't require a huge initial investment in equipment. Start small, with the basics, and leverage items you already have and expand as your business grows.

Pots and Trays

Starter pots are small pots or trays that typically have individual cells used for starting seeds or rooting cuttings. They are generally inexpensive and reusable. If you do plan to take cuttings from your plants or start seeds, you'll likely need to invest in starter pots or trays.

Grow-out pots may be needed if you plan to raise your plants to larger sizes before selling. As plants develop, they will need to be transferred to larger pots to accommodate their growing root systems and you'll need to have grow-out pots ready. The size of these pots will vary depending on the mature size of the plant, and how long you plan to nurture and grow your plants before selling.

Depending on your business model, you might also need decorative pots. Decorative pots can increase the aesthetic appeal of your houseplants and potentially increase sales. There is a world of options available to create or repurpose decorative pots. Do your research and consider the plant's health and proper growth requirements if you plan to sell your plants potted in decorative pots. The pot should be appropriately sized to accommodate the plant's root system, and it should provide enough space for the roots to grow and expand without being cramped. The pot should have drainage holes at the bottom to allow excess water to escape. Proper drainage is crucial to prevent water-logged soil, which can lead to root rot and other moisture related issues. Pots are available in various materials and each material has different properties, including insulation, weight, and breathability. Consider the specific needs of the plant and the impact your pot could have on total weight if you plan to ship it after sale.

Plant Propagation Supplies

A good pair of clean, sharp pruning shears is also essential for taking cuttings without causing unnecessary damage to the parent plant.

Rooting hormone can help stimulate root growth in cuttings, increasing propagation success rates. Rooting hormone should be in your supply cabinet!

Growing medium, whether you choose quality potting mix or propagation media is essential for healthy root development. (Propagating in water is also an option.)

Labels and markers will be critical for keeping track of what you're growing, especially when dealing with multiple plant varieties.

A heat mat, though not critical, can provide consistent warmth to aid in the rooting of cuttings, or growth of young plants, especially important to consider for tropical or warm climate plants.

Humidity Domes or Mini Greenhouses can come in handy to help maintain the higher humidity environment that many cuttings need to root successfully.

Growing and Maintenance Supplies

Pots and containers in various sizes will likely be needed for planting and growing out plants.

Quality Potting Soil that is suitable for the specific needs of the plants you are growing is a must have.

Potting Mix will help you as your plants grow larger and begin to need a more substantial growing medium. Potting mix usually contains a combination of peat moss, compost, perlite or vermiculite, and sometimes also a slow-release fertilizer.

Specialized soil mixes might be needed if you plant to raise plants that require specific soil conditions. For instance, succulents and cacti prefer a fast-draining soil mix, while orchids require a very light, bark-based mix. You'll need to carefully select your soil mix to match the needs of the plants you are growing.

Fertilizer will be needed to provide your plants with the nutrients they need to grow healthily. There are many types of fertilizer available, so choose one appropriate for the types of plants you're growing, and their individual needs.

A watering can or hose or other system will be essential for watering plants during both the propagation and growth stages.

Spray bottles for misting young cuttings and plants are also handy to have around.

Grow Lights are additional optional items that can be helpful if natural light is limited. You may need to consider these under special circumstances.

Plant care and Maintenance Supplies

Pruning tools including pruning shears, scissors, or other tools for maintaining plant shape and health and taking cuttings should be in your supply arsenal.

Depending on the scale of your operation, a watering system such as drip irrigation or a misting system may eventually be necessary.

Pest control products such as insecticidal soap, neem oil, or other pest control solutions to manage pests and disease will be needed long-term.

Business Essentials

If you plan to ship your plants, you'll need appropriate packing materials: boxes, labels, padding, tape, and protective materials for shipping houseplants safely and securely.

You will also need some basic record-keeping tools, ideally a software system for tracking inventory, sales, and expenses. You don't need to get too fancy initially; a simple Excel spreadsheet might be all you need.

If you plan to sell plants online or at markets, consider branding materials, signage, and packaging to promote your business. Depending on your specific plans, you also may need tables, chairs, a secure cash box or even a pop-up tent to support a market presence.

7 BRANCHING OUT: BUSINESS STRUCTURE AND LEGAL CONSIDERATIONS

The first few months of Lily's foray into selling houseplants on eBay and Etsy had been a whirlwind of activity, with evenings full of packaging orders. Images of her carefully nurtured plants had attracted green-thumbed buyers, eager to bring a piece of her botanical paradise into their own homes.

However, the journey hadn't been without its thorns. Shipping live plants had proven to be a delicate dance of timing and packaging. Despite her meticulous efforts, a few leaves occasionally seemed to arrive bruised or pots broken, leaving her with a couple dissatisfied customers and refund requests. This was tough, especially since she was still a relatively new seller on these platforms and didn't have hundreds or thousands of reviews to insulate her from the blow of a negative mark. The learning curve for shipping plants proved to be steep, and the stress weighed heavily on her.

Determined to root her business in more stable ground, Lily set her sights on the local farmers' market—a hub right around the corner from her apartment where the community gathered each Saturday to enjoy local produce and crafts. It promised direct engagement with plant customers and the joyous absence of shipping woes.

Lily looked up the sponsors of the event online and inquired about securing a booth, only to uncover a new layer of complexity. She needed to first be an official business. She needed a business tax ID. It was a step she hadn't anticipated, but as she gazed at her plants reaching towards the sunlight, she too felt a pull towards growth.

This realization marked a turning point. Lily knew that if she wanted her business to flourish, she would have to plant it on firmer legal ground. It was time to transform her casual online sales into a legitimate enterprise.

The following Saturday she headed to the market and asked a woodworking vendor how he got started. He told her about the local Small Business Association (SBA) and shared that that is where he went for guidance on how to create a comprehensive business plan and information about how to officially form his business. He said they also offer trainings and workshops that had helped him address the exact topics Lily was facing, as well as many other challenges.

On her lunch break from her office day job the following Monday, Lily visited the Small Business Association. There she met a kind gentleman who shared several resources, including on demand information available on their website. She also learned that they regularly offer workshops and seminars on various aspects of running a business, such as marketing, finance, legal issues, and technology, which Lily recognized could be invaluable to her professional development.

Their website was especially helpful. It provided a comprehensive summary of everything she needed to officially start, grow, and expand her business. Unlike some of the general resources she had scanned online about forming a business, she really liked that these resources were specific to her location. Laws, the agencies an entrepreneur may need to work with, and tax structures vary by state; Lily found that having a local resource available to help her through the necessary processes specific to her location was extremely helpful. Armed with this information, Lily made a list of the forms she would need to fill out in order to obtain the necessary permits and licenses.

The next chapter of our journey involves navigating the maze of business licenses, tax forms, and the nuances of becoming a recognized entity. While Lily found it to be a daunting process, the seed of her entrepreneurial spirit had been sown, and she knew this was necessary for her business to bloom.

Business Structure

As Lily started the journey to legitimize her houseplant venture, she spent time learning about business structure options that were available. There are choices available, and each is appropriate in different circumstances. Do your research and consult with professionals and trusted mentors to ensure you select the business structure that will work best for you in the long run.

Sole Proprietorship

This seemed to be the simplest form of business under the law, with no distinction between the business and the owner.

Lily learned that as a sole proprietor, starting her business would be as simple as continuing what she was doing but under a registered business name and with a business license.

The administrative burden was minimal – way less paperwork and it was the lowest cost option she researched. A sole proprietorship would also give her direct control of all decisions. The downside, however, was that it came with unlimited personal liability, meaning if the business incurred debt or got sued, her personal assets could be at risk.

Limited Liability Corporation

Next, she considered a Limited Liability Corporation (LLC). This structure offered nearly the same logistical ease of a sole proprietorship. An LLC could protect her personal assets from business debts and claims, a feature that greatly appealed to Lily as she thought about future potential growth.

It did, however, require more paperwork than a sole proprietorship with a little extra cost. She would need to file articles of organization with the state and draft an operating agreement. The maintenance involved annual fees and periodic filings, but it seemed manageable.

S-Corporation

The third option Lily found was an S-Corporation (S-Corp), a special designation that allowed profits to pass through to her personal tax return, avoiding the double taxation often associated with corporations. She learned that S-Corps were more complex to set up and maintain. An S-Corp would require scheduling meetings, documenting minutes, and generally adhering to more formalities.

While this option provided tax benefits along with the benefit of limited liability, the administrative and regulatory requirements were significantly greater than those of an LLC.

C-Corporation

Lastly, Lily looked into a standard Corporation (C-Corp). This structure was an independent legal entity, separate from its owners, providing the strongest protection against personal liability. However, the complexity of forming a corporation was daunting. It required extensive record-keeping, documenting operational processes, and also came with potentially higher administrative costs.

Additionally, corporations faced double taxation—first on the company's income and then on any dividends paid to shareholders. This seemed excessive for her modest operation.

Permits and Licenses

After weighing her options, Lily decided to invest some of her recent business profits to form a limited liability corporation (LLC). She completed the required paperwork, paid a filing fee and soon, her official company, which she named "Houseplant Root LLC" had been formed!

Lily felt that forming an LLC struck the right balance for her between protecting her personal assets and minimizing paperwork, and that this would allow her to focus on what she loved most—nurturing her plants and growing her business.

Lily's careful review of the materials she received from the Small

Business Association not only helped her align on an LLC as the right structure for her, but also helped her understand that there were other permits and licenses she would need.

In addition to beginning the process of establishing her LLC, she learned that to sell in her area, she needed to apply for a General Business License. And after reviewing a farmers' market Vendor Guide that the Small Business Association provided, she realized she would need a Special Event Sales Tax License in order to sell items locally at a temporary event like a farmers' market, as well as insurance.

Lily's trip to the Small Business Association helped her understand that her state's Department of Agriculture has specific regulations regarding the sale of plants. In her state specifically, Lily learned she needed to apply for a Nursery Stock Dealer License.

Lily's mind was swirling with all the forms and applications she needed to complete. Once again, to keep on track, she made a list of each application and form she would need to submit. It was intimidating at first, but during the next month, she worked through the process one form at a time and completed each application.

Lily kept detailed notes and maintained her checklist which helped her keep tabs on the status of receiving all necessary applications and permits.

Small business owners do need to do due diligence to ensure they understand the types of permits and licenses required. Unfortunately, there's no easy singular answer to this question since permits and license requirements vary by location. Here are some common types of permits and licenses that could be required in your area:

Business License

Nearly all businesses in the U.S. require a basic business license. These are typically issued by the city, county, or state where the business operates. A business license grants a business permission to operate legally within the specified jurisdiction.

Nursery License

Some states require a nursery license for businesses that sell plants, including houseplants. Whether this is required or not varies by state, and in some cases is only necessary if the business expects to achieve a certain volume threshold of sales. A nursery license is typically regulated by the state's Department of Agriculture. Its purpose is to ensure that the business adheres to agricultural standards and meets any state requirements for plant health inspections. It's advisable to check in with your state's Department of Agriculture to understand when a nursery license might be needed and the requirements to obtain and maintain licensure.

Sales Tax Permit

If your business sells goods directly to consumers within a state that collects sales tax, you will need to obtain a sales tax permit. This permit allows the business to collect sales tax on taxable sales. Platforms such as eBay and Etsy typically manage the collection of state sales tax on behalf of sellers, however, as you venture into local community sales or even selling through your own website, it will be crucial to obtain a sales tax permit and to collect sales tax in accordance with the laws of your state.

Home Occupation Permit

It isn't universally required, but in some jurisdictions, businesses that operate out of the business owner's home may need a home occupation permit. This permit is designed to ensure that the business's activities comply with local zoning laws and do not disrupt other neighborhood residents.

Environmental Permits

In some cases, large scale businesses may require additional environmental permits. These involve regulations related to water usage that require a special permit, waste disposal, or the use of pesticides.

How to Figure it All Out

There are resources who can help you understand, for your location and your business specifically, what types of licenses and permits might be needed for your city, county, or state.

- The U.S. Small Business Administration's website www.sba.gov offers a wealth of information on federal and state level licenses and permits. You can find this information in the "Licenses and Permits" section of their site. This is a great resource to set you on the path of understanding what may be required.

- Your local City Clerk's Office and County Clerk's Office are also typically able to provide information about local business licenses and permits required in your area.

- Your state's Department of Agriculture will be able to confirm any requirements for obtaining a nursery license. They can also help you understand any additional agricultural regulations that might apply to your business.

- Your state's Tax Department can help you understand sales tax permits. In many cases, state department of revenue or taxation websites provide guidelines on registering a business for sales tax collection.

- Finally, consider obtaining professional legal advice. There is so much variation across states, and in some cases, there is even variation within a state. Navigating complex state regulations can be challenging. Depending on your area and your comfort level researching this type of information, in many cases it may be a prudent decision to consult with a legal professional who specializes in business law. This is often the easiest way to obtain highly tailored advice and ensure that you have all the necessary documentation in place.

Ultimately, compliance with local, state, and federal regulations is crucial for operating a houseplant business legally and successfully. However you choose to navigate this process, it's important that you take the time to research and obtain the correct permits and licenses. A little work up front can save you from potential fines and legal issues down the line.

Regulatory Considerations Selling Plants

Early on when looking at other plant listings on eBay and Etsy, Lily noticed the listings often included states that the seller wouldn't ship to.

This is because several states in the U.S. have regulations and restrictions on shipping houseplants. These rules are intended to prevent the introduction and spread of pests, disease, and invasive species. California, Florida, Arizona, Hawaii, and Texas each have restrictions that regulate the importation of plants and plant products.

The restrictions vary by state but generally include plant quarantine regulations and very specific requirements for shipping plants into each state.

Lily had her hands full completing the required paperwork to establish her business's legal entity and be able to sell plants locally. She decided that the right choice for her business would be to immediately review all her Etsy and eBay listings and ensure they noted that she was unable to ship to California, Florida, Arizona, Hawaii, or Texas. With each sale she made, she would verify the address of the buyer and if they were in one of these states, she would cancel the order, refund their purchase, and send them a note to explain.

While deciding for the time being not to ship plants into these states, Lily is interested in reviewing the requirements for each of these five states and evaluating whether she could meet their requirements in the future.

If she can meet the requirements, being able to sell houseplants in some or all these states could be a valuable future niche market to explore. Many sellers are intimidated by the complexity of navigating additional restrictions, so a seller who is able to be successful in some or all of these states would have less competition and potentially could gain a large, loyal customer base.

States that Restrict Plant Shipments

It's important for a houseplant side hustler to understand restrictions that apply to shipping plants to California, Florida, Arizona, Hawaii, and Texas. As a new seller of plants, it may be easiest to establish a policy that you do not ship to these states. However, there is tremendous market potential for sellers willing and able to navigate regulatory complexity and pursue options to ship to these states.

8 A GARDEN OF OPTIONS FOR SELLING PLANTS

Lily's hard work paid off, and the day finally came - Houseplant Roots LLC had successfully secured each and every permit and license needed! The process was at times a test of patience, but with each form she submitted, and each approval stamped, Lily's confidence blossomed.

With all legal necessities behind her, Lily finally secured a spot at the local farmers' market. The night before her debut, she carefully selected an array of her best specimens. She gathered a folding table and sunshade that she had borrowed.

The next Saturday morning proved to be clear and bright, a perfect day for marketgoers to come enjoy fresh, local produce and artisan goods. As she arrived at the farmers' market, the woodworker who she had first asked for advice about how he got started greeted her with a warm smile, and she learned his name was Herb. Herb was an incredible craftsman who was selling handmade cutting boards, chess boards and wood trinket boxes. She also met an affable woman named Clara who was selling handcrafted pottery at the booth next to her. Clara had a bright smile and was a skilled artist who sold the most beautiful, handmade dinnerware that Lily had ever seen. Both Clara and Herb were experienced farmers' market sellers. They were incredibly welcoming to Lily and offered to help her with any questions she might have.

The market closed as the sun set and Lily raced home and counted her earnings. She recognized that the true profit of the day was the community she had cultivated and the newfound friendships that had sprouted with Clara and Herb.

All the work she had completed to legally formalize her business had brought her to this watershed moment, infusing her with a newfound legitimacy and expanding her horizon of opportunities. Selling at the farmer's market was not just a milestone; it was a gateway to a realm of possibilities that Lily had only begun to consider.

She was excited to head back to the farmers' market the following week, and also eager to identify additional potential venues where she could sell her plants. Everywhere she went, she saw future possibilities. Each café, boutique, and local business she visited sparked visions of consignment opportunities. Lily's imagination ran wild as she dreamt of future pop-up plant shops at art galleries, yoga studios and even co-working spaces. The allure of seasonal markets and garden fairs was another avenue Lily was eager to explore. Her eyes had been opened to new possibilities. Nearly everywhere she went, she saw a future potential venue for selling her plants.

Selling Houseplants Across Many Venues

There are probably as many avenues for selling plants as there are varieties of houseplants! From the far and wide reach of e-commerce platforms, like eBay and Etsy, to a personal touch at a local farmers' market or festival, there are many possibilities. What's even better is that these options are really just the tip of the iceberg! With an open mind and creative approach, the world around you is full of unique and creative opportunities. This includes some less obvious options too, like selling plants on consignment in coffee shops, antique stores, or other local establishments. Or maybe you'll find that embracing the communal spirit and selling plants at local plant swaps, or via community bulletin boards is right for you. Whether you're just sprouting your business idea or looking to branch out, there are many venues available to help you sell your houseplants.

Online Marketplaces

E-commerce platforms such as eBay, Etsy and Amazon provide a convenient way to reach a large audience of potential buyers. You're able to create listings with a minimal time investment. With the right photos and descriptions, you can start selling plants and cuttings today. There are other online marketplaces devoted specifically to plants, such as Plantly.com and Blossm.com. This is all in addition to options such as Facebook Marketplace, Craigslist and even Reddit.

Social Media Platforms

Social media platforms such as Instagram, Pinterest, Facebook, and X (formerly Twitter) are great options to showcase your houseplants and engage with potential buyers, while building a community. You can create posts, stories, and share live videos that highlight your inventory, all while engaging a natural platform for interacting with prospective customers.

Local Plant Sales and Farmers' Markets

Like our friend Lily, you may have local farmers' markets, craft fairs, or plant swaps in your area. Setting up a booth at one of these events can be another great option for selling your plants locally and having an opportunity to directly engage with your customers. You could even consider organizing a plant swap in your community and charging a registration fee to other interested plant sellers!

Plant Shops and Nurseries

Local specialty plant shops or nurseries are another potential sales avenue. You could consider selling these establishments large quantities at reduced, wholesale rates. This is a helpful way to sell large quantities of plants, while only needing to invest in building and maintaining a limited number of relationships, with only the plant shop and nursery buyers, rather than engaging and providing customer support to all downstream customers.

Consignment Plant Sale Opportunities

Have you ever been to a coffee shop and admired a beautiful selection of plants in decorative containers that provide ambience for the establishment and are offered for sale? Pursuing consignment opportunities with local businesses is yet another way you can sell your plants. Consider coffee shops, bookstores, antique stores, gift shops, galleries, and other possible options you may have in your area. Your plants can help the shop owner create a more welcoming environment for customers while providing you an opportunity to reach new customers!

Local Classifieds and Community Boards

You can even post a message offering your houseplants for sale through local ads. Whether these are physical bulletin boards in your community, low-cost newsprint classified ads or online neighborhood social media sites (like, local Craigslist or Facebook Marketplace postings), this can be a great way to connect with local buyers in your area. As added benefits, you might just meet some new friends who live close by, and you won't have to worry about shipping your plants!

Deciding on Sales Channels that Work for You

When deciding on the combination of sales channels that will work for you, consider what you can manage as well as the buying habits of your target market. By diversifying your sales channels, you can experiment with different options and maximize exposure for your inventory.

9 FROM GREEN LEAVES TO GREENBACKS: HOUSEPLANT PRICING

Lily had her plants, each one a leafy, green bundle of potential profit, but there was a question looming over her, "How much should she really be charging for each?" Her initial approach was simply to be competitive with other sellers. She would find a similar plant online, and price hers at the same price or slightly lower. She knew it was time to dive into the world of pricing strategies to understand if there was a better way.

With a steaming cup of herbal tea in hand and her laptop in front of her, Lily began her research expedition. Her first stop? Online forums, social media groups, and e-commerce platforms. She scoured these sources, noting the prices of plants that were similar to hers. She compiled a list that included each type of plant she had in her collection. She made notes of the prices that others were charging, the size and health of the plants offered, what was being charged for shipping and any added value like fancy pots or care instructions that came with the purchase.

Armed with her research, Lily sat down to crunch the numbers. She began to realize that pricing wasn't just about covering costs and making a modest profit; it was about telling a story. She wanted her prices to reflect the care, knowledge and love she poured into each one of her plants. She saw that sellers who were telling stories and adding information were creating value that was reflected through higher prices.

Lily decided to experiment with a few pricing structures. For her more common plants, she'd remain with her competitive pricing strategy, keeping her rates on par with or slightly below the average market price to attract first-time buyers and stand out in a more crowded market. For the rare specimens in her collection, she'd go with value-based pricing, setting higher prices that mirrored the plant's uniqueness and the sheer joy they brought to plant enthusiasts.

But Lily's pricing adventure didn't stop there. She wanted to add a sprinkle of fun. She introduced "Happy Hour Plant Sales," where she'd offer discounts on certain plants for a limited time each week on her website. She even toyed with the idea of "Mystery Plant Bundles," where customers could purchase a surprise selection of plants at a fixed price, adding an element of excitement to the shopping experience while giving her flexibility to best manage her inventory.

To gauge her customers' reactions to her pricing strategies, Lily decided to use social media polls and direct feedback from her sales. She was open to tweaking her prices based on customer responses and sales trends, treating it as an ongoing adventure rather than a set-in-stone decision.

In the end, Lily realized that pricing her plants was less about finding the perfect number and more about connecting with her customers, understanding their needs and desires, and offering them value that went beyond the price tag. And with that realization, Lily felt more confident than ever in her houseplant side hustle.

Considerations When Pricing Houseplants

As a houseplant entrepreneur, understanding and implementing effective pricing strategies is crucial to the success and sustainability of your business. Pricing strategies not only influence your profitability but also how your brand is perceived by customers. When setting prices for houseplants, several factors should be considered, including the type and size of the plant, its rarity or demand, the effort, and resources you invested in propagation as well as market trends. There are some guidelines for setting prices for new cuttings, rooted cuttings, and mature plants.

When pricing rooted cuttings, consider how established the root development is. Rooted cuttings that have well established roots and are ready for planting should be priced higher than younger cuttings. Larger or more developed rooted cuttings should command higher prices, especially if they're close to maturity and will require less time to grow into mature plants. Be prepared to adjust your prices based on demand for the specific plant variety you are offering and the availability of similar offerings in the market.

The considerations for mature plants are similar. Again, you'll want to consider the size and maturity of the plant. Larger plants with well-established root systems and substantial growth should be priced higher to reflect their advanced stage of development. Plants with rare or unique characteristics (variegation, unusual growth patterns, specific coloration, etc.), can command premium prices due to their rarity and desirability. Healthy thriving mature plants should be priced higher than those with signs of stress, damage, or poor growth. Consider the value of any special decorative pot that is included. Finally, market value and demand vary greatly by plant type. Research the current market value for mature plants of the same variety and adjust your pricing based on demand, scarcity, and competition.

As you strengthen your brand message and support offerings, ensure your price points are adjusted to reflect the totality of what your customers are receiving, not simply the financial value of the plant or cuttings. For example, will you include care sheets with your plants, decorative plant identification tags? Do you offer a full refund "no risk" purchase to your buyers to help compensate for plants that don't survive the journey? Do you offer your buyers strong customer service or additional plant education opportunities? These and other value-add services provide your customers with a level of confidence when buying from you and differentiate you from competition. With the right presentation of how you add value above and beyond the plant itself, you can command a higher price point.

There are several pricing strategies available. Gaining a high-level understanding of each approach, and a sense of when it might be appropriate to test that message can bolster your business's margins and set you up for long-term success. There are some common pricing strategies to consider in different scenarios:

Cost-Plus Pricing

This is a straightforward strategy that involves adding a fixed percentage or markup to the cost of procuring or producing each plant. It's a simple way to ensure all costs are covered and a profit is made. This strategy is most appropriate for entrepreneurs who have a very clear understanding of all their costs and wish to maintain a consistent profit margin across products.

Competitive Pricing

Competitive pricing involves setting prices based on what competitors are charging for similar plants. This is the strategy Lily innately practiced by researching what comparable plants were selling for and offering her plants at or slightly below that amount. A competitive pricing strategy requires that you regularly monitor the market to remain competitive, without undercutting your own potential profit margins. This pricing strategy is typically seen in highly competitive markets where price plays a crucial role in customer decision-making.

Value-Based Pricing

Value-based pricing is an assessment based on the perceived value of your plants to the customer, rather than an objective cost of the plant itself. This strategy can allow for higher profit margins, especially if your plants are rare, of exceptional quality, or you are providing added services such as personalized care advice. Value-based pricing is ideal for entrepreneurs who offer unique plants or exceptional customer service that adds value in the eyes of their customers.

Psychological Pricing

Psychological pricing leverages customer psychology to encourage purchases. You'll often see items priced just below a round number (e.g., $9.99 instead of $10). This strategy plays on a common perception that slightly lower prices are better deals. It's particularly effective when you are attempting to encourage impulse buys or when you want to make a price point seem more appealing to customers.

Penetration Pricing

Penetration pricing involves setting lower prices to enter a new market or gain a quick share of an existing market. The prices you set in this strategy will usually be increased once you've captured market share. This strategy is appropriate for new entrepreneurs trying to establish themselves in a competitive market.

Premium Pricing

Premium pricing is a technique whereby prices are set higher with the intention that a higher price point reflects high quality or exclusive plants that aren't available elsewhere. This strategy is suitable for businesses offering rare, exotic, or high-end houseplants that appeal to a niche market who is willing to pay more for perceived value and quality.

Dynamic Pricing

Dynamic pricing is a strategy where an entrepreneur adjusts their prices in response to market demand, competitor prices or even other external factors. This is a flexible approach that is increasingly used in online sales and can help entrepreneurs maximize profits during high-demand times. To be done right, dynamic pricing requires sophisticated software or diligent market analysis.

Regardless of the pricing strategy or strategies you deploy, test market tolerance for different price points and adjust based on your results. Be sure to regularly review and update your prices based on market trends and customer feedback to help ensure your prices remain competitive and reflective of the full value you offer.

10 FROM SEED TO BOX: SECURE AND EFFECTIVE HOUSEPLANT SHIPPING

Lily had been energized by her initial farmers' market experiences and the world of possible sales channels she now saw before her. She reflected on the journey that had brought her to this point. She thought about how her frustration with shipping plants led her to a tangled web of paperwork and permits, and then ultimately to the official formation of her business. The lesson was clear and profound: every problem was solvable, a challenge to be met with the same patience and care that she gave her plants.

Lily had learned that growth, both personal and professional, was much like tending to her garden: it required time, attention, and a willingness to sometimes dig through dirt to find solutions.

Recognizing that every problem was solvable, she began to view her previous eBay and Etsy shipping challenges through new eyes. She set her sights on mastering the art of shipping her plants and cuttings. She knew that with the right research, dedication, and experience, she could improve her eBay and Etsy sales, and she wasn't going to let her early frustrations with shipping drive her away from reaching customers across the country.

She started by looking closely at other sellers of houseplants. She scoured the feedback they had received from buyers and zeroed in on every mention of their shipping and packaging practices. She reviewed their shipping policies and she eagerly watched and rewatched the unboxing videos that some sellers include in their listings. She gained valuable insight into common challenges and steps a seller can take to maximize their odds of success.

From positive comments that had been left about the packaging and shipping of plants, Lily identified theme areas that she felt she could immediately apply to improve her own shipping practices.

- Sellers who used expedited shipping options had happier customers.

- Buyers who left positive reviews often referenced the seller's choice of eco-friendly materials.

- Beautiful packaging was more than a nice to have, it was something buyers appreciated and that seemed to set some sellers apart from others.

- Lily also saw firsthand just how valuable it was when a seller included an unboxing video in their listing. These sellers were able to visually tell a story about the care they took with their plants. The videos demonstrated securely packaged plants and happy customers who were delighted to open beautifully packed boxes and unveil lush, healthy plants. Lily immediately recognized the power of unboxing videos to help build excitement and anticipation for the customer, while also setting the right expectations for the role the customer would play helping their plant acclimate to their home.

Lily also learned from negative reviews.

- First, she observed that plants and cuttings needed to be securely packaged. Plants that arrived damaged or cuttings with broken stems meant unhappy customers.

- Second, any shipping delays during the process could hurt

plants and frustrate customers. Such delays also damaged the seller's ratings, even when the delay seemed to be out of the seller's control.

- Extreme weather has the potential to damage plants in transit. Sellers who shipped plants in severe weather events without packing them in a way that effectively mitigated the environmental challenges were at risk of receiving negative feedback from buyers.

Lily also explored the shop policies of her competitors. She observed that sellers with positive reviews often specified certain days of the week when they shipped live plants. These were typically early in the week and intended to minimize potential carrier delays over the weekend and holidays.

Setting the right expectations for buyers was important to help customers be successful. Successful sellers included educational material with their plants to help the buyer acclimate the plant to its new surroundings. They also worked to proactively help their buyers understand that the plant might need a few days to recover from its journey before it begins to thrive.

Lily also observed that some sellers who sell houseplant cuttings require that their buyer purchase multiple cuttings to enhance the chances of success. For other sellers, based on reviews Lily gathered that the seller shipped multiple cuttings, even when the buyer purchased just one. When comparing the price points of these two types of sellers, it seemed to even out. One group of sellers offered lower price cuttings, but required multiple purchases and another group of sellers charged a higher price point and appeared to ship multiple cuttings. In either scenario, providing multiple cuttings was clearly a technique to increase the chances of at least one cutting successfully taking root and thriving, leaving a happy customer and healthy plant.

How to Ship Houseplants and Cuttings

Start with a healthy, well hydrated plant. For cutting, ensure there is healthy new growth.

Hydrate plants and cuttings before shipping. Make sure plants are well-hydrated before packaging them for their big trip. Water plants thoroughly, while being careful not to waterlog the growing medium. The goal is to help the plant maintain a healthy moisture level during transit.

For cuttings, wrap the cut end in a damp paper towel or sphagnum moss to keep them moist. Spritz cuttings with water. Then, wrap the entire cutting in plastic wrap or place it in a plastic bag to prevent it from drying out.

Ship Multiple Cuttings to Increase Your Customers' Success

If one cutting fails to take root or experiences issues during transit or while settling into its new home, your customer will have additional cuttings as backups. Providing multiple cuttings demonstrates a commitment to customer satisfaction and increases the likelihood of a successful transaction.

Minimize the Potential for the Plant to Move in Transit

A great way to do this with cuttings is to place them securely in a small box, and then place this first box in a larger, second box. Use tissue paper, bubble wrap or other packing material to cushion the inner box and minimize movement.

It's important to secure a potted plant for shipping to ensure that both the plant and its pot arrive at their destination undamaged. Like when shipping cuttings, a box within a box is an option to secure plants during the shipping process.

Another option is to use a flat piece of cardboard to secure the potted plant within your shipping box. To do this, start by selecting a box that is just slightly larger than the potted plant. Next, take a flat piece of cardboard that is the same dimension as the inside of your shipping box. Cut a circle in the center of this piece of cardboard that is slightly smaller than the diameter of the pot. Make small relief cuts around the radius of the circle (without cutting all the way to the edge of the cardboard). Place the narrow end of the pot into this cardboard ring and slide the cardboard ring up the pot until it is secure.

Place packing material at the bottom of your shipping box. Then, carefully fit your plant with its cardboard ring into the box. Fill any empty space with packing material. The cardboard ring, properly secured around your pot, will minimize the plant's movement during shipping.

Include instructions in the box to help the recipient welcome their new plant or cuttings. These should include general instructions on how to acclimatize a plant to its new surroundings, as well as any plant-specific care instructions. Also include your contact information and encourage buyers to contact you directly if they have questions or issues.

Secure the box with packing tape. Clearly label the package as "Live Plant" and include a "Handle with Care" or "Fragile" label.

Help Your Plants Arrive Quickly

Choose an expedited shipping method that ensures the cuttings will arrive quickly, ideally within two to three days. Choose a service that offers tracking and delivery confirmation.

Ship early in the week to minimize the chance that your plant or cuttings might sit in transit over the weekend.

Advanced Shipping Options for Certain Circumstances

You may need to consider additional special handling options if you are shipping from an extreme climate (either hot or cold). When adjusting for seasonal extremes, or if you plan to sell plants that are highly sensitive to temperature or humidity fluctuations, this is also key.

One great option is to ship using insulated packaging materials, such as foam inserts or insulated boxes which can help maintain a stable temperature inside the shipping container. This can help protect the plants from temperature fluctuations during transit.

Depending on the weather conditions and the temperature requirements of your plants, consider using heat packs or cold packs to further regulate the temperature inside the shipping container. Heat packs can provide warmth during cold weather, while cold packs can help keep the temperature lower in hot conditions.

Packaging materials that can help retain moisture such as sphagnum moss, moist paper towels, or breathable plastic bags can help maintain a humid microclimate around your plants during shipping. For delicate cuttings or seedlings, you might even want to consider using humidity domes or clear plastic covers to maintain higher humidity levels within the shipping container. This can help prevent desiccation and wilting of the plants during transit.

While it's important to maintain humidity, it's also crucial to provide adequate ventilation and prevent the buildup of excess moisture inside the shipping container, which can lead to fungal growth or rot in some plants. You can achieve this by cutting air vents or holes in your shipping box, or the inner box or shipping materials that are holding your plants.

There are options to minimize the movement of plants during shipping, help them maintain tolerable temperature and humidity levels and provide adequate ventilation. Learning how and when to use each method is both art and science. Regularly monitoring feedback from buyers is important for your ongoing learning. If necessary, adjust your packaging, such as by adding more moisture-retaining materials or adjusting ventilation.

Eco-Friendly Packing Material

In the green and growing world of houseplant entrepreneurship, adopting eco-friendly packaging practices isn't just a nod to sustainability, it's a powerful statement that can truly differentiate your business in the eyes of an environmentally conscious customer base.

If you choose biodegradable pots, recycled or recyclable boxes, and packing materials that leave minimal environmental footprints, you're not only doing your part to protect the planet but also appealing directly to customers who value eco-conscious practices. This approach not only elevates your brand in terms of your commitment to environmental responsibility but can also make you an appealing choice for customers who are eager to support businesses that align with their values. In essence, eco-friendly packaging can become more than just a way to deliver your plants; it reflects your commitment to sustainability and a greener future, setting your plant business apart in a really good way.

If you are interested in exploring eco-friendly packing materials, there is an ever-growing array of options available.

These include biodegradable and compostable pots made from materials such as coconut coir, rice hulls or peat. These pots can be planted directly into the soil, reducing waste, and minimizing the use of plastic. Consider using recycled or biodegradable paper packaging for wrapping plants, or even consider creating your own repurposed packaging materials from paper shred. Biodegradable packing peanuts are another popular and sustainable option. Eco-friendly cushioning materials are available as alternatives to traditional plastic bubble wrap; these include materials made from recycled paper, corrugated cardboard, and biodegradable air pillows.

If there are elements of your shipping that seem to truly require plastic, fear not; plant-based plastics are now options. There is an increasing range of bioplastics made from renewable resources like cornstarch and sugarcane that can be viable choices if you need plastic bags or plastic protective sleeves as part of your shipping practices.

When you need to tie something in place, like securing a bag around a young plant's stem, rather than synthetic ties or twine, try using natural fiber options. Jute, hemp, cotton and even wool are excellent biodegradable and compostable options. An added benefit is that these natural elements add a beautiful touch to your packaging!

Regardless of your chosen path through eco-friendly packaging material, embrace minimalism in your packaging design. Use only the material that is necessary and focus on simple, recycled, recyclable and biodegradable options. This will help you to save on shipping supplies! Your plants, your customers and the planet will thank you.

Post-Delivery Service to Help Plants Thrive in Their New Homes

As Lily refined her packaging and shipping strategies, she realized that delivering her leafy companions safely to their new homes was only part of what her customers needed. She was committed to ensuring her plants thrived in customers' hands, long after the unboxing excitement had faded. Lily shifted her focus to setting her customers up for post-delivery success, transforming them from novices to confident plant parents.

Lily started this process by making sure her contact information was impossible to miss. She included it on every care sheet, order confirmation, on her boxes and within the package itself. At every step, she invited customers to reach out with questions. Each plant she shipped was accompanied by a detailed care sheet that was tailored to that plant's specific needs. These sheets covered everything from the optimal light conditions the plant needed to the watering schedule and preferred humidity levels for it to thrive. She gave her customers a handy guide right from the start.

Taking her commitment a step further, Lily attached a tag to each plant, summarizing its basic care requirements and providing its common and botanical names. This small but significant touch meant that even if the care sheet was misplaced, essential information was still readily available, hanging right on the plant itself.

And Lily didn't stop there. She developed an email template, filled with helpful tips, which she sent to customers immediately following the delivery of their plants. This email not only confirmed the safe arrival of their new green friend but also reiterated the plant's care needs and reminded customers that Lily was just an email away for support. It also served as a friendly reminder that their live plant had arrived and encouraged the customer to unbox the plant as soon as possible.

Through these thoughtful actions, Lily empowered her customers to become successful plant parents. Her holistic approach to customer care helped forge a deeper connection between her business and her customers, turning one-time buyers into loyal fans of her brand.

Helping Customer Acclimate their New Plant

Helping your customers acclimatize their plant to its new home is easy to do and can help you build a strong brand identity, while also minimizing potential for negative customer reviews.

Consider sending an email to your customer when their plant arrives. This is an opportunity to demonstrate your care for the plant and that you care about the customer's satisfaction. It also invites the customer to contact you directly if they have an issue or questions. This email outreach is a great opportunity to help your customers understand the steps they can take to safely unbox their plant and help it adjust to its new home.

Your instructions to your customer detailing how to unbox the plant might include reminders to gently remove any packing materials, ensuring that no part of the plant is trapped or crushed. The email might encourage them to carefully inspect the plant for any signs of damage or dehydration. If their plant appears dry, recommend an initial light misting of the foliage to provide immediate hydration.

To help your customers succeed, educate them with best practices to help their new plant acclimate. Help your customers understand that it's common for a plant to show signs of stress from a big trip. Houseplants might show signs of wilting or drooping when they first arrive. Even taking great precautions while shipping plants, it's possible that the plant may have some damaged leaves, stems, or flowers, due to handling during shipping. Suggest that your customers place a new plant in an initial location with indirect light and consistent, moderate temperatures. Recommend that your customers avoid placing plants in direct sunlight or extreme environmental conditions immediately after unpacking. Help your customers understand what to do over the course of several days to a week, such as gradually exposing the plant to increasing amounts of light and introducing watering.

At first, Lily's houseplant side hustle seemed straightforward—grow plants, sell them online, and ship them to other plant enthusiasts. However, the reality of wilted leaves and damaged stems forced her to delve into the world of shipping methods. She learned about temperature control, humidity packs, and the importance of sturdy, yet breathable packaging. Lily realized that the 'when' was just as crucial as the 'how'. She began timing her shipments to avoid weekend delays, ensuring that her leafy parcels spent the least possible amount of time in transit. She also improved her customer support following the delivery of a houseplant by offering them meaningful guidance to help their new plants acclimate.

With each tweak and adjustment, Lily not only improved the journey of her plants but also rekindled the flame of her own passion. The online feedback in her eBay and Etsy shops started changing. Customers were not just satisfied; they were delighted. Photos of healthy, thriving plants started to flood her inbox, with glowing reviews showing healthy plants on sunny kitchen windowsills, and kind words about the care she took to package and ship their plants.

Lily saw her sales on eBay and Etsy surge. Her virtual storefronts became bustling markets, repeating throughout the week the success she was seeing Saturday at her physical stall at the local farmers' market booth.

However, with booming business came a new challenge: demand was outpacing supply. Her existing plants, which she had nurtured with such care, could barely keep up with the orders. It was a good problem to have, but a problem, nonetheless. Lily realized it was time to scale up.

She started researching different houseplant varieties she could possibly add and brainstormed other options, like managing supply and demand by establishing a 'Plant of the Month' subscription service. And she couldn't help but wonder if her business could be even more successful if she were selling directly to her online customers, through her own website.

As each new idea came to her, she would jot it down in her notebook. And her little notebook was quickly filling up. To build on her success and to pick the most impactful next steps she could take to help her business grow, she needed to transform these ideas into an actual business plan.

11 CULTIVATING A DREAM: SETTING GOALS AND CREATING A BUSINESS PLAN

As Lily's mind and notebook overflowed with ideas, she realized she would need a more strategic approach to sustain and nurture her business's growth. While she had already accomplished the foundational tasks of establishing her LLC, obtaining the necessary permits, and setting up shop on eBay and Etsy, as well as selling locally at the farmers' market, she understood that her entrepreneurial journey was just beginning.

The next phase of her venture required careful planning and a clear vision of the future. That's when Lily turned her attention back to the resources provided by the Small Business Association (SBA). The SBA offered a wealth of information and tools designed to help small business owners like Lily set goals, plan, start, manage, and grow their businesses.

Lily attended business workshops and webinars, where she gained insights into effective goal setting, business planning, marketing strategies and financial management. She took advantage of the SBA's free counseling services, sitting down with experienced mentors who helped her refine her ideas and set realistic goals.

With their guidance, Lily established goals and started drafting a business plan—a roadmap for her company's future. This process helped her articulate her vision. She wanted to expand her online presence with a dedicated website. She wanted to be able to offer a plant subscription service, a feature that would provide a steady income stream and build a committed customer base, while also improving her own ability to predict demand and ensure adequate supply. She also wanted to explore the feasibility of introducing new and exotic plant varieties to her collection, a move that could set her apart from competitors.

The business counseling services she received helped Lily understand that, although it was not yet scribbled in her notebook, she needed to learn about marketing activities, and she needed to develop an intentional approach to marketing.

Lily used this planning process to prioritize her ideas based on their potential return on investment (ROI). She examined the costs associated with each initiative, the resources required, and the expected timeline for seeing results. Through this analysis, she determined that while building her own website would require an upfront investment, it would save her money in the long run by reducing the fees she paid to third-party platforms. Furthermore, it would give her more control over the customer experience and the flexibility to implement her vision of a subscription service.

For her website to be effective, she needed to build out a marketing plan to ensure that its content reflected her business's voice and was appropriately tailored to her target market. Having a solid marketing plan would guide not just the development of her website's content but would help her understand all touchpoints she has with her customers and guide her in how to craft compelling messages and campaigns that would increase sales.

The subscription service idea was identified as a high ROI initiative. It promised not only recurring revenue but also the opportunity to build a more personal relationship with her customers. It would encourage repeat business and provide a predictable sales forecast, which would be instrumental in managing her inventory and cash flow.

Introducing new plant varieties was another idea that Lily was passionate about. However, her business plan helped her recognize that this should be a more gradual process. She decided to start small by adding just a couple new plant species that were in demand and known *for their hardiness during shipping. She would fulfill her personal desire to learn about new plants with these specimens, while not overinvesting in this aspect of the business too early on. Over time, she would continue learning about different plants species, and would expand gradually, or if buying opportunities presented themselves.*

With a better idea of her goals and a business plan in place, Lily felt confident about the future. She had a clear set of priorities, a deeper understanding of her financials, and a strategic approach to expanding her business.

Goal Setting

Whether you are content with a small houseplant side hustle that brings in modest supplemental income or if your hope is to one day scale your business, it's important to set goals, monitor your progress and evolve as needed. Setting realistic goals for a houseplant side hustle isn't difficult but does involve some planning and that you have a clear understanding of your resources, the market and your personal strengths and limitations.

Assess Your Starting Point

Take stock of what you already have—your initial capital, the space available to you for growing or storing plants, your existing plant collection, your knowledge of horticulture, and the time you can dedicate to this venture. This will help you understand your current capabilities and will help you gain clarity about areas where you may want to focus on developing to help support your business growth.

Conduct Market Research

Understand the demand in your target market. Look into what types of houseplants are popular, what price points are feasible, and who your competitors are. When you pass community bulletin boards in your area, or visit a local farmers' market, look closely for others who might be selling houseplants, and assess whether these could be future avenues for you to market and advertise your plants.

There's plenty of room in the houseplant market for your venture to be profitable alongside existing sellers. Remember that demand for houseplants is both high and increasing. Don't be intimidated by competition – but do learn from it.

By carefully studying the marketplace, you'll be able to develop compelling listings for your plants and price your plants appropriately. And through this process, you just might identify a niche that might be underserved, such as rare plants, easy-care varieties for beginners, or sustainable organic houseplant options.

Financial Planning

Think about your financial goals for your side hustle. How much profit do you aim to make monthly?

Are you looking to cover a specific expense, save for a goal, or do you want to turn this side hustle into a full-time business? Your objectives will shape your financial goals. Take time to understand your current financial situation and your business objectives. Look at your income, expenses, savings, and debts. This will help you determine how much additional income you need or want from your side hustle.

Keep in mind that you will need to reinvest some of your profit back into the business for it to grow. Set a realistic budget that includes all costs: plants, soil, pots, tools, marketing, and any additional help you might need. Budget for necessary expenses like materials, advertising, or software subscriptions that will help you grow your business. These costs should be factored into your financial picture.

Start Small and Scale Gradually

If you're new to the business, you may want to follow Lily's model and begin with a small, manageable inventory. Test the waters with your chosen market and scale up as you understand demand patterns and your capacity to meet them.

As you achieve success, consider then adding more types of plants or testing different product offerings.

Achieving Aggressive Financial Targets

If you are setting aggressive financial goals for yourself, keep in mind that achieving them will likely require more time and effort than modest initial goals.

Aggressive financial targets will likely mean you'll need to increase your output, sell more plants, perhaps sell through multiple venues, which directly translates to more hours of work.

You may need to quickly develop new skills or improve existing skills to meet demand or to offer higher-value products or services. Generating more business may require more marketing and networking, which can be time-consuming but is essential for growth. To handle the increased workload without burning out, you'll need to find ways to work more efficiently. This might mean investing time in learning new tools or automating parts of your business.

Set SMART Goals

Regardless of your specific objectives, you'll be more likely to achieve them if you translate your objectives into goals that are Specific, Measurable, Achievable, Relevant, and Time-Bound (SMART). For example, rather than a vague goal like "sell more plants," a SMART goal might be "sell 20% more succulents each month for the next quarter."

Check up on your progress frequently and adjust your goals when needed.

If you have a large financial goal, break it down into smaller, more manageable milestones. For instance, if your goal is to earn $60,000 in a year, break it down to $5,000 per month, and then consider what weekly or daily income targets that would translate into.

By building out time-bound goals, you'll be able to create a clear timeline for your business. You should also break your goals into short-term and long-term objectives with clear deadlines. For example, decide by when you will have your inventory ready, or when and how you will first offer your plants for sale. Set goals with dates to identify when you expect to reach each goal.

Here are a couple common areas you should think about when first starting a side hustle. Consider building goals that align to some or all of these common side hustle priority areas. Reflect on your priorities and objectives in each of these areas, and other areas that are important to you. This activity will help you focus on the most impactful work you can complete to reach your goals.

Goal for Acquiring and Retaining Customers

Decide how you will reach your customers. Will you use social media, local markets, word of mouth, or will you collaborate with other local businesses? This is about identifying your audience and determining how best to reach them. Set specific, measurable time time-bound goals related to acquiring and retaining customers.

A couple example goals in this area might look like:

- "Sell 20 cuttings on Etsy by the end of Quarter 2."

- "Introduce myself and my business, by sharing contact information and following up with 20 new people I meet at this weekend's plant swap."

Goal for Your Own Education and Growth

Aim to continuously learn more about houseplant care, the latest trends, and general business management. Set goals for enhancing your knowledge and skills, which in turn can help grow your business.

Example goals in this area might look like:

- "Read 2 plant care books a month."

- "Attend 3 small business seminars in Quarter 3."

Work-Life Balance

Since this is a side hustle, it's important to consider setting goals that allow you to maintain a healthy balance between your main job, your side hustle, and your personal life. Avoid overcommitting yourself to the point of burnout.

Example goals in this area might look like:

- "I will work on my side hustle every Tuesday and Thursday evening from 6:00 PM to 9:00 PM, and Saturday mornings from 9:00 AM to 1:00 PM, totaling 10 hours per week to ensure a clear separation between work and personal time."

- "By the end of next month, I will reduce my hands-on involvement in non-core activities by hiring an assistant for 5 hours per week, enabling me to concentrate on growing the business while preserving personal downtime."

Monitor and Adjust

Regularly review your goals and your progress. Be prepared to adjust as you gain more insight into the business. Flexibility is key, especially when dealing with unexpected challenges and opportunities.

By setting realistic goals that are tailored to your unique situation and target market, you'll be better equipped to build a successful houseplant side hustle that can grow over time. Remember that success doesn't happen overnight, and patience and persistence are just as crucial to nurture as your plants.

Creating a Business Plan

Creating a business plan can be a helpful exercise for any entrepreneur. It's a roadmap that outlines the direction, goals, and strategies of a business, serving as a guide for decision-making and growth.

The business plan should be considered a living document, regularly reviewed and updated as the business grows and changes. It serves as a valuable tool, not just for the startup phase, but throughout the life of the business, helping to keep it on track and aligned with its current goals. You'll notice, however, that Lily didn't pause her entrepreneurial endeavors until she had a business plan in place. She was actively selling through e-commerce platforms and the farmers' market before she ever contemplated a formal business plan.

In fact, oftentimes, just like Lily, for many entrepreneurs, it makes more sense to build momentum by just getting started where you are with what you have. Gradually as your business grows and you've had a chance to try it out and validate that this venture will work for you, there will come a point where you'll recognize that a business plan can help you prepare for the next phase.

This book is not a definitive guide to writing business plans. There are far more robust books, online resources, and other tools available that accomplish that task. This section simply provides a high-level overview of the components of a typical business plan.

Executive Summary

This is a brief overview of the business, including its name, location, the product or service it provides, and its mission statement. It also outlines the business's objectives and its strategies planned to achieve them.

Company Description

This section provides detailed information about the business. It includes the legal structure, ownership, and a brief history. It also typically includes the type of market the business serves, and the business's advantages over competitors.

Market Analysis

Here, an entrepreneur provides information about the industry, target market, and competition. This includes data on market trends, customer needs and behaviors, and a detailed analysis of competitors.

Organization and Management

This outlines the business's organizational structure and management team. It includes details about the legal structure, an organizational chart, and profiles of the management team.

Products or Services

This section describes the product or service the business offers. It should explain the benefits provided to customers, the product life cycle, and any intellectual property rights or special services.

Marketing and Sales Strategy

This is the business's plan for attracting and retaining customers. It outlines the pricing strategy, promotion, distribution, and sales strategy.

Funding Request

If the business plan is being used to secure investment, this section provides a detailed explanation of the funding required, how it will be used, and the terms the entrepreneur is prepared to offer.

Financial Projections

This section provides an overview of the business's financial health. It includes income statements, balance sheets, and cash flow statements. It also typically provides a forecast for the next five years.

Appendix

This is an optional section that includes any additional

information, such as resumes, permits, or contracts.

The business planning process helps prioritize the next steps for a business by providing a clear picture of the current situation and future goals. Each section of the plan serves as a steppingstone towards achieving the business objectives.

The market analysis, for example, can help identify potential opportunities or threats, guiding current and future decisions about which products or services to focus on. The marketing and sales strategy can help prioritize which promotional activities to implement first.

12 FROM SOIL TO SALE: UNDERSTANDING AND DEFINING YOUR HOUSEPLANT NICHE

Through the goal setting and business planning process, Lily realized that she needed to build a marketing plan to help Houseplant Roots LLC effectively reach her target customers. And first, she needed to gain clarity on just who those target customers really were by defining her niche. To guide this activity, she started by writing a SMART goal. She wrote:

> *"Specific: I will conduct comprehensive research to identify two new niche markets within the indoor plant industry that my business can target. I will gather data on market trends, customer preferences and competitor strategies. Based on this research, I will develop a detailed marketing plan that is tailored to each niche.*
>
> *Measurable: My success will be measured by identifying at least two underserved niches and developing a marketing plan for each.*
>
> *Achievable: I have allocated one week to complete my initial research. Outside of my day job, I have cancelled outside*

commitments to ensure that I am able to invest the time necessary to complete this work. I have identified steps that I will take to define my houseplant niche markets.

Relevant: By targeting niche markets, I can create more effective, personalized marketing campaigns that stand out against competitors. This approach is in line with the immediate priorities that I identified for my business during the business planning process.

Time-Bound: I will complete my niche market research within one week and have the marketing plans ready to be executed within one month. This timeline includes one week for initial research and identification of niches and three weeks for developing my marketing plan."

This SMART goal will help Lily stay focused on the task of identifying lucrative niche markets and creating a strategic marketing plan to reach them, with clear benchmarks for measuring progress and success.

When beginning her research into niche houseplant markets, Lily began by reflecting on her entrepreneurial journey to date and carefully considering commonalities of her past and current customers. She recalled that she initially, by observing her friends, had recognized that many people wanted to bring greenery into their homes but were uncertain of where to start. Lily's initial plant sales were for easy to care for, low-maintenance plants that were ideal for novices. These "starter" plants were not only forgiving and easy to care for, but they also provided her customers instant gratification.

Lily also considered her personal long-term desire, that as her business grows, she wants to push the limits of her plant care expertise and cultivate more rare plants. These plants will cater to a different segment of the market: collectors and plant aficionados. Her rare plants will attract a premium price from a targeted customer base that is willing to invest more in unique and uncommon plants.

Through her business journey, Lily learned the importance of *identifying and serving a niche market. Focusing on specific segments will allow her to tailor her marketing strategies effectively. For beginner plants, she has already started providing care guides, easy-to-understand tips, and robust customer support to help new plant owners feel confident. For the rarer plants, this information will be basic to her already plant savvy customers, and her marketing to this niche will need to emphasize the uniqueness, rarity, and quality of her plants.*

These targeted approaches will inform Lily's sales strategies as well. Beginner plants will require a different sales message—one that reassures the customer about the ease of care and resilience of the plant. In contrast, selling to collectors will require highlighting the plant's pedigree, rarity, and potential as an investment.

Her customer service will also need to be adapted to each niche. For beginners, she will focus on providing education and support, including detailed instructions, and she will be available to answer questions. For collectors, she will emphasize the health of the plants and that the plants were shipped with extra care; she also plans to provide authenticity certificates for her rare varieties.

Find Your Niche in the Houseplant Market

The good news for a budding houseplant entrepreneur is that there are too many houseplant niche markets to name, and more cropping up daily! Get started in your houseplant side hustle by selecting a targeted niche market or two to dive into and test.

Choosing a niche will help you focus on a specific type of customer and their needs. This clarity will help you determine the best venues to reach your target customers, and it will inform your decisions about what houseplants to offer and how you might market your products.

Let's jump right in and explore some potential houseplant niche markets for you to consider.

Beginner-Friendly Houseplants

Like Lily, you could opt to start your business by catering to beginner plant enthusiasts. With younger generations interested in houseplants, there are more beginners looking to build a plant collection now than ever before. Consider catering to this demographic by selling easy-to-care-for houseplants. Choose plants that beginners may find appealing due to their low maintenance needs.

You'll likely notice more competitors in this space, but don't let that deter you. The beginner houseplant market is robust, and the needs of beginner plant keepers present a wide range of opportunities for offering products and services in addition to plants. For example, you could offer starter kits that include cuttings, pots, soil, and other planting essentials. You could sell related products such as planters, tools, and care products. Like Lily, you could aspire to build a subscription service designed to help beginners build a plant collection by sending different cuttings or plants each month.

And you could consider catering to beginner needs by offering educational content and providing strong customer service. While excellent customer service can differentiate your business and encourage repeat purchases, regardless of the specific niche you choose, if you are catering to beginners, providing educational and supportive customer service is an especially valuable way to differentiate your brand.

If you think that catering to houseplant beginners could be for you, here are just a few easy to care for houseplants that are beginner-friendly and worth considering.

- **Pothos (Epipremnum aureum):** Tolerates low light conditions and irregular watering – perfect for a beginner who might still be developing a habit of basic plant care in their daily routine.

- **Snake Plant (Sansevieria):** This plant almost thrives on neglect! It can handle both infrequent watering and low light, once again making it an ideal option for newbies.

- **Spider Plant (Chlorophytum comosum):** Adapts to a variety of conditions and is easy to propagate.

- **ZZ Plant (Zamioculcas zamiifolia):** This is a very hardy option. The ZZ Plant plant survives droughts and low-light situations, making it beginner-ready.

- **Peace Lily (Spathiphyllum):** Tolerates low light and can help beginners learn to care for plants by providing visible signs, namely drooping leaves, when watering is needed. This makes it a great teacher for beginners; it is a plant that can actually help teach basic plant care skills!

- **Jade Plant (Crassula ovata):** A succulent that requires minimal water and can live for many years.

- **Philodendron:** Similar to pothos, with a variety of shapes and sizes, this is yet another houseplant option that is known for forgiving inconsistent care.

- **Lucky Bamboo (Dracaena sanderiana):** Grows well in water or soil and requires little light.

- **Aloe Vera:** A hearty succulent that requires little watering.

- **Heartleaf Philodendron (Philodendron hederaceum):** A trailing plant that thrives in various light conditions.

Rare and Exotic Plants

Maybe you're a seasoned houseplant expert with rare, sought after plants adorning your windowsill. Do you have the necessary skills and passion for providing a more precise level of care that is highly tailored to a specific type of plant? If so, raising rare and exotic plants can also be a lucrative endeavor.

Collectors and enthusiasts are willing to pay premium prices for rare and exotic houseplants. These plants aren't always easy to find and, depending on the plant, they may have very specific environmental or care requirements in order to thrive.

Being successful raising rare and exotic plants does require a solid knowledge base or a desire to dig deep and learn about very specific plant types and the care they require. This niche is suitable if you have a true passion for unique plants and you are willing to invest in their proper care.

If the idea of raising rare plants appeals to you, here are just a few examples of plants you might want to learn more about:

- **Variegated Monstera Deliciosa (Monstera deliciosa 'Variegata'):** This plant has large, glossy leaves with distinctive holes and irregular white or yellow variegation. The variegated variety is much rarer than the common green Monstera and can fetch a premium price.

- **Pink Princess Philodendron (Philodendron erubescens 'Pink Princess'):** This philodendron is coveted for its pink variegated foliage. Each leaf is unique, with splashes of pink, dark green, and sometimes white.

- **Variegated String of Hearts (Ceropegia woodii variegata):** This trailing vine has heart-shaped leaves with striking variegation. It's popular in hanging baskets and can also fetch high prices; this is especially true for well-established plants.

- **Rhaphidophora Tetrasperma 'Mini Monstera':** While not a true Monstera, this plant has similar split leaves and is sought after for its compact size and rapid growth. Variegated forms of this plant are particularly rare and command high prices.

- **Anthurium Clarinervium:** Known for its velvety,

heart-shaped leaves with bright white veins, this anthurium is a collector's favorite. It is not only rare but also slow growing, which adds to its value.

- **Variegated Alocasia (Alocasia macrorrhizos 'Variegata'):** This plant has large, arrow-shaped leaves with striking variegated patterns. The variegation can be unstable, which makes high-quality specimens especially valuable.

- **Philodendron Spiritus Sancti:** One of the rarest philodendrons, this plant has long, narrow leaves. It is native to a small area in Brazil. Due to its rarity and demand among collectors, it can also command extremely high prices.

- **Encephalartos Woodii:** This is a cycad rather than a traditional houseplant, but it's worth mentioning due to its rarity and price. Native to South Africa, it's extinct in the wild, and only clones from a single male specimen exist, making it one of the rarest plants in the world. Think of how amazing it would be to not only raise this plant, but to be a part of preserving clones from the last specimen known to exist!

- **Hoya Carnosa 'Compacta Variegata' (Variegated Hindu Rope):** This hoya has twisted, waxy leaves with creamy white or pink variegation. It's a slow grower, which can make large, mature specimens quite costly, but it will also require time to grow them out to this point.

- **Queen Anthurium (Anthurium warocqueanum):** Known for its long, dark green leaves that can reach several feet in length, the Queen Anthurium is a highly sought-after decorative plant that commands high prices.

You'll notice a theme throughout this list, the rarity and price of these plants comes from factors like difficulty of propagation and slow growth rates. You'll also notice that this list includes many plants with interesting or rare variegation, where care needs may be more modest or novice-friendly; for these plants the rarity factor is driven by the plant's unique genetic characteristics.

If you are expanding your plant collection to include rare plants, be cautious of where you purchase your plants, as there have been some issues with illegally trafficked plants. Protect your business and always opt to work with reputable sellers who acquire and propagate plants ethically and legally.

Eco-Friendly and Sustainable Plants

Or maybe environmentally conscious consumers appeal to you and are your target market? If you're interested in reaching this growing customer base, consider eco-friendly and sustainable plants. Focus on growing organic, locally sourced plants, and using biodegradable packaging. Highlight your eco-friendly and sustainable business practices in your marketing to appeal to these customers.

This niche could be right for you if you're passionate about sustainability and if you desire to create a brand around it.

Theme Shoppers, Subscription Services and Kits

There's a growing trend in subscription services and DIY kits related to houseplants. These offers cater to the convenience and experiential shopping preferences of modern consumers. The services could include not only the plants themselves but also pots, soil, and care instructions, making it easier for beginners to enter the hobby.

Beginners and gift buyers flock to both kits and themed plant offerings. Creating themed plant kits could be right for you if you enjoy curating collections and creating experiences.

Themed plant offerings could include seasonal holiday plants.

Which could be plants that are typically popular during holidays, or maybe plants cut in a topiary shape that mimics a mini-Christmas tree, or even plants packaged with an assortment of festive ornaments that the recipient can use to decorate. Other themes to explore could include bundling plant cuttings with pots, soil, and instructions as part of a 'Plant Transplanting Kit!' Or a similar offering with seeds and instructions for how to grow a plant from the very beginning. Or, the themes of your kits could be based on plant benefits, like air-purifying plants, or aesthetic themes, like a "desert vibes" succulent kit.

The options are absolutely endless! If marketing themed plant offerings feels right to you, a little brainstorming will undoubtedly yield dozens or more additional ideas.

Pet-Friendly Plants

Pet owners who are also plant enthusiasts are a perfect niche to provide a curated selection of plants that will not harm pets if ingested.

To be successful in appealing to this audience, you first will need a thorough understanding of pet-safe plants. But the good news is, with just a little research, this is a very attainable knowledge base to build! From there, building a brand that promotes and highlights your greenery as pet-friendly can be an excellent niche if you love animals and want to ensure their safety.

Edible Plants

Culinary enthusiasts and health-conscious individuals create a perfect market if you're interested in selling edible or medicinal plants.

Consider offering a variety of herbs, small vegetables, or fruit-bearing plants that can be grown indoors. This could be a good fit if you're also into cooking or urban farming, or are knowledgeable about medicinal plants.

Community and Education

There is a robust community aspect to houseplant ownership,

with forums, blogs, and social media groups dedicated to sharing care tips and their plant experiences. This community-driven market supports a demand for workshops, books, and courses on plant care.

There are tons of opportunities if you're interested in teaching plant care classes locally, or even offering online classes or other educational content to reach a broad, nationwide (or even worldwide!) audience.

Gift Economy

Houseplants make popular gifts. They make a sustainable and longer lasting token of affection than traditional flower bouquets. They're often given for housewarmings, office openings, and as thoughtful gestures for friends and family. Marketing your plants to a specific gift occasion can help you appeal to customers who might be searching online for gift ideas. Examples might include Sympathy gifts, Birthday, Mother's Day, Easter, Hostess Gifts, Teacher Gifts, and many, many more options.

Specialty Plants and Rare Specimens

Then, there's the ever-in-demand niche market for rare and exotic plants. These plants can command high prices among collectors and enthusiasts. This segment of the market is particularly lucrative and has its own dynamics and considerations. If you are truly passionate about plant care and the idea of being a steward of a rare plant is appealing, this could be a great fit for you.

Urban Gardening and Food Plants

Beyond ornamental houseplants, there's also a demand for plants that can be grown indoors for food, like herbs, small vegetables, and fruit-bearing plants. This ties into the farm-to-table movement and a common desire to grow one's own food, even in limited spaces. An especially interesting option here could be raising and marketing indoor food plants that also have elements of traditional indoor ornamental houseplant décor appeal. There are tons of possibilities, but a few examples could be providing beautiful potted kitchen herbs, or a planter of beautiful mixed salad greens, or even a potted ginger plant that the new owner could later harvest and enjoy!

Seasonal Offerings to Boost Revenue

Another potential niche (or series of niches) to consider is seasonal offerings. If you have space to rotate and prepare small crops for seasonal plant sales, this can be a great way to stand out at markets and festivals and to draw in new customers. Perhaps what appeals to you is starting pots of vibrant mums that you can sell as the quintessential fall crop, or nurturing tulips to brighten your collection in spring, or even grooming topiaries into festive, unconventional Christmas trees! It is possible to rotate plant crops based on their seasonal appeal and bring horticultural variety to your life, while planning in advance for revenue boosting seasonal best sellers. With the right planning you can anticipate and prepare for seasonal demand, while super charging your side hustle.

Beyond fall mums, spring tulips and mini evergreen Christmas displays, there is a wide range of options to boost your seasonal appeal. Amaryllis bulbs produce stunning, trumpet shaped flowers in a variety of colors and are popular during the winter holiday season. Christmas cactus with its colorful flowers in shades of pink, red or white bloom in late fall to early winter and add a welcome burst of color to cold months. As the name suggests, Easter Lilies are popular at Easter and known for their large, fragrant white flowers. Hyacinth is a wonderful fragrant, spring blooming bulb that comes in a range of colors and are popular for their beautiful, dense clusters of flowers. Daffodils are another cheerful spring blooming flower with bright yellow or white petals. The large, sunny blooms of sunflowers are always popular at the end of summer and in the early fall months and bring a burst of cheer to indoor spaces.

An interesting thing to think about when considering seasonal offerings is that the limited time they're available can actually be a strong psychological motivator for customer purchases. The "fear of missing out" (FOMO) factor that seasonal, limited time offers generate can help maximize your sales. The seasonal aspect of the products creates a sense of psychological urgency in buyers by subtly emphasizing that the products are available for a limited time only. This can help maximize sales.

Plant Resell Opportunities

Reselling houseplants is another often overlooked houseplant niche. People move all the time, and lugging mature houseplants rooted in heavy pots full of soil is not always an option. It is possible to buy houseplants at garage sales, estate sales or to find them at a very low cost (sometimes even free) and then resell them for a profit! This can be a viable way to source inventory for a houseplant business as well. This is especially true if you have knowledge of houseplants and can identify valuable or desirable species.

Look for healthy, well-maintained houseplants and be very careful in your examination. You'll want to ensure you're not inadvertently introducing pests or diseases that could hurt other plants you have. This doesn't mean you need to overlook imperfect plants, but you should be cautious and understand what you are getting into. Plants that have sustained some neglect can be great opportunities to purchase at a bargain price, nurse the plants to health and resell them for a hefty profit. In fact, some overgrown plants actually present a unique opportunity for you to practice your plant division skills and maximize your potential profit by turning one overgrown plant into two or more resalable products!

Never lose sight of the resale value of a plant. Be willing to walk away if the purchasing price is too high or if you see signs of pests. Factor in the cost of any necessary maintenance or repotting you may need to do.

Guidance on Selecting a Niche

Whether you're interested in one of these niche houseplant

market suggestions, or if you have identified a separate niche, it's wise to thoroughly think through your target market. Put yourself in their mindset and consider the products that will appeal to them, marketing messages that will resonate with them and logistics of how you will reach them.

Do your research. Look into what's trending, what's available in your area, and where there might be a gap in the market. Evaluate demand by using tools like Google Trends or social media to gauge interest in your chosen niche.

Analyze your skills and passions and pick a niche that aligns with what you're good at and what you enjoy doing. If you are happy creating plant products for a certain niche, you'll be more likely to stick with it and achieve success.

Consider the logistics of how you will reach your chosen niche. Are there existing online forums where you can connect with them, or groups where you can reach them directly in your local community? Will you need to ship products to reach your audience, or will you sell locally?

Wherever you choose to start, keep your target customer top of mind. Develop products and services that they will enjoy and seek out. Create and refine your marketing content to meet their needs.

13 PHOTOSYNTHESIS OF IDEAS: BUILDING A MARKETING PLAN

After identifying beginner plant keepers as her primary niche market, and rare plant enthusiasts as a smaller and future state niche market she wished to explore, Lily began thinking through how to market and sell to these customers. Putting her newfound planning skills back to work, she put pen to paper once again. This time her sights were set on creating a comprehensive marketing plan that would help her focus her efforts and effectively reach and engage her audience.

Lily's evolution from houseplant hobbyist to business owner had happened quickly. She was selling online, and at the farmers' market before she had really thought through her brand's identity. She realized that to help her deliver a memorable customer experience she needed to have a logo and clear brand identity developed for Houseplant Roots LLC. Lily opted to outsource this activity, and she found a graphic designer on Fiverr with experience building strong visual brands. She shared her vision for establishing a memorable brand identity that appealed to an audience of beginner houseplant keepers, but that was also broad enough to appeal to an experienced plant enthusiast community in the future.

The outsourcing of this work yielded fast results which included a well-designed logo, color palette, and even some sample branding messaging that she might leverage throughout her marketing materials.

Even though she hadn't yet begun building a website, her initial focus on beginner plant keepers as a primary niche helped her outline potential website content that would draw in this audience. Recognizing that beginner plant keepers often seek guidance, Lily decided she would create a "Plant Care 101" section. This section would include blog posts and articles on basic plant care, how to diagnose and address common plant problems, and other tips for success. By providing valuable, targeted content, she aims to attract her primary audience to her website and establish her brand as a trusted source of information.

Of course, she also thought about website content that would help her drive online sales. This would include engaging photos of lush, green plants, and compelling descriptions that were tailored to help beginners feel confident that they could appropriately care for each plant. There would also be an easy-to-use, secure checkout process available for her customers.

Through her research, Lily had also learned that beginner plant keepers tend to be very active on social media. She researched the platforms they were most engaged on and identified Instagram and Pinterest as the primary social media channels she would use to reach her target audience.

In her marketing plan, she documented a strategy for regularly posting high-quality images of her plants, behind-the-scenes peeks into her growing plant operation, and plant care tips.

Furthermore, to build a loyal customer base, Lily decided to start a weekly email newsletter. She would encourage website visitors to subscribe to her newsletter by offering a one-time discount on plant purchases. Her subscribers would then receive plant care tips, new product announcements, exclusive discounts, and previews of blog posts.

Within each plant box that she shipped, Lily was already including some basic care instructions. She decided that she would improve the aesthetics and content of her care guides and would also add a prominent QR code to her guides. This would help her new customers easily find her website.

She also realized that there was an opportunity to humanize her business and connect more deeply with recent customers by including a handwritten thank you note with each purchase.

Finally, Lily thought more about the exterior of her plant packaging. She wasn't ready to invest in pre-printed boxes with her logo, but she identified custom rubber stamps and stickers as lower cost alternatives that would let her deliver a stronger brand presence on her packaging.

She researched her options and factored into her marketing budget the costs of creating and printing enhanced plant care guides, custom thank you notes, branded rubber stamps and stickers.

Lily also thought she could draw more customers into her booth by using eye-catching signage at her farmers' market stall. Her farmers' market stall signage would also include a QR code, again leading to her website. This would allow potential customers to learn more about her business, subscribe to her newsletter and view additional plants that she had available for sale.

After building out her comprehensive marketing plan, Lily was eager to start creating content and felt that she had built a strong outline that would enable her to effectively reach her primary niche.

Building Your Own Marketing Plan

After you've identified your niche market, leverage everything you know about your target customer to build a marketing plan that will help you reach them.

Again, there are plenty of resources available with robust information about what a marketing plan can and should include. This is a simple summary to help point you in the right direction.

At a high level, you'll use your marketing plan to outline your niche market and begin documenting your opportunities to engage with them through content and other outreach.

It may be helpful to produce customer personas, or detailed profiles of your target customers that include demographic information, interests, behaviors, and motivations. These personas can keep you focused on the needs of your target audience and help you develop marketing strategies and tactics that will resonate with your audience.

Of course, the specific strategies and tactics you'll use to achieve your marketing goals should also be documented in your marketing plan. This could include an outline of content you'll create, social media plans, email marketing, educational resources you'll include with the orders you ship, QR codes you might create to drive website visits, labelling on packaging that will drive brand recognition, and more.

With a clear picture of the marketing strategies and tactics that you plan to deploy, you'll be able to estimate the budget that will be required. A detailed breakdown of your marketing budget, including how much you plan to spend on each marketing activity will help you balance your investments across your business and understand and plan for likely future expenses.

Your marketing budget should also factor in potential challenges or obstacles you might face during the implementation of your plan. Include enough cushion in your budget to help you navigate unforeseen challenges.

Finally, just like your business plan itself, your marketing plan should be a living document. You should regularly review and update it, as necessary, to reflect changes in your business environment, customer behavior, target niche, products offerings, or company objectives.

Creating a Custom Unboxing Experience on the Cheap

You can use your packaging as an opportunity to create a lasting experience with your customers without breaking the bank! In fact, creating a custom-branded unboxing experience can be quite affordable. A plain box can be easily transformed into a memorable first encounter with your brand with the assistance of custom-made rubber stamps that feature your logo and contact information. Eye-catching custom stickers are another affordable option. These simple touches not only elevate the unboxing experience you are delivering, but also weave your brand's identity into every package you send out.

If you're at the starting line without a brand logo, no worries! Platforms like Fiverr offer low-cost outsourcing options. You can connect with talented designers and branding experts today for minimal cost. In no time, you can have a professional brand image that makes an impact!

14 UNLOCKING A DIGITAL GARDEN: BUILDING A WEBSITE AND MORE

Lily's business planning process helped her identify that building a website that would allow her to sell directly to customers was a high value activity. Lily had no experience designing websites and was overwhelmed thinking about where to start. But she leaned into her newfound business planning skills and realized that she needed to start with a goal. She once again found herself building a SMART goal to guide her toward her website's successful creation and launch. In her notebook, she wrote:

> "Specific: I aim to create a branded e-commerce website for my plant business that will feature a user-friendly interface, detailed product descriptions, customer reviews and will offer a secure checkout process. The website will also be equipped to handle a future planned plant subscription service, which will ultimately help me cultivate recurring sales.
>
> Measurable: To measure the success of my website, I will track the number of visitors, conversion rate, the total number of subscriptions sold, and customer feedback.
>
> Achievable: I have researched affordable online platforms that will allow me to build and maintain my own website. I have

spoken with other entrepreneurs who have used similar platforms, and I am confident that I can follow in their footsteps. I have also allocated part of my budget to acquire a domain name and to fund my website's maintenance.

Relevant: Building a website is essential for my business. It will reduce my dependency on third-party platforms and increase my profit margins, all while providing a more personalized shopping experience for my customers. This step aligns with my long-term goal of expanding my online presence and establishing a direct channel to my customers.

Time-Bound: I plan to have the website go live within three months. This includes one month for planning and design, time for development and testing, and another month for final revisions and launch preparations."

By following this SMART goal, Lily is confident that she can focus her efforts and resources effectively, making the task of launching a website a more structured and manageable process.

After exploring the various website creation platforms and services available, Lily decided that Shopify would meet her needs and would allow her the flexibility she desired for her future subscription service. Its interface, e-commerce features, capability to add a blog and reasonable pricing were in line with her business needs and her budget. With this decision made, she went ahead and secured her domain name, www.houseplantroots.com.

Lily was pleasantly surprised by the simplicity of setting up her website. She found the platform to be intuitive to initially build her content, add listings, and go live. She appreciated the platform's pre-designed templates and drag-and-drop features, which allowed her to create an appealing and functional website without specialized knowledge.

While pleased to have it up and running faster than she thought possible, she quickly realized that her website would be an ongoing project. It would require regular updates, improvements, adding fresh content and new listings. While her website did not include every piece of content she had planned from the outset, Lily understood that it was a work in progress, and she was okay with that. She was excited about the prospect of gradually adding more information, products, and features that would further enhance her customers' experience.

She could add a blog to share her love of plants and hopefully help her share her knowledge with a wider audience. Who knows, maybe there would be future affiliate marketing program opportunities if she included affiliate links in blog posts about products that she recommended, or maybe even future opportunities to include sponsored content or targeted advertising. There were so many possibilities!

Lily was particularly proud of the speed at which she had managed to create her e-commerce platform. If her marketing tactics and strategies were successful, this website would significantly reduce the need to share her profits with third-party platforms like eBay and Etsy, which charged much higher fees for using their services. She could offer her customers the same plants at a lower cost, while realizing more profit in the process!

There was still plenty of work ahead, but Lily was confident and excited about her new venture. She looked forward to the journey of growing her business through her very own website, continually improving it to meet her customers' needs while also achieving her business goals.

Tips for Building Your Own Website

Embarking on a journey to create your own website might sound like a really big, scary project, especially if you're not well-versed in coding or web development. The good news is that we live in the most amazing times, and with the right platform, you don't need website development experience to create a thriving online space. With the right tools and attitude, you can create a captivating digital presence.

The content possibilities are virtually endless. You could use your website to share plant care wisdom, engage with a community of fellow enthusiasts, as well as to offer your plants for sale. It's true, all of this and more is possible through a website that you've designed and crafted yourself. The process may sound complex but fear not; you're about to discover a user-friendly path that requires no special knowledge. The beauty of the digital realm is that it welcomes creators from all walks of life. Your passion for plants is the only fertilizer that is needed for this endeavor! So, let's break through the digital soil, and watch as your online garden blooms into a vibrant haven for plant enthusiasts worldwide.

Selecting the Right Platform

There are many platforms available if you're interested in establishing your own online storefront. At the moment, Shopify, WordPress with WooCommerce, and Squarespace are popular choices that offer a balance of usability, customization, and e-commerce capabilities. Of course, there may be additional options available, and it always makes sense to explore all options before making a decision.

There are some factors you should keep in mind to help you compare services and make an informed decision about the platform that will work best for you.

First, like Lily, it's important that you have a clear view of your website's purpose, the type of content it will deliver, whether you too plan direct-to-customer sales, and any anticipated future expansion, such as Lily's idea of expanding into a plant subscription service.

Unless you have experience building websites, choose a platform that is user-friendly, and designed for web development novices. Look for intuitive interfaces and drag-and-drop functionality. You also should explore the support resources available if you do run into challenges.

If you plan to include educational content or blog posts, you'll want to prioritize platforms that make it easy to publish and organize these types of articles.

And it's really important that the platform you choose is ready to support online sales! Ensure the platform supports e-commerce functionalities, including secure payment gateways, inventory management, and order processing.

Look for platforms that offer customizable templates that match the aesthetic of your brand. Consider whether the platform provides enough flexibility for you to customize your website to reflect your brand identity without the need for extensive coding.

You'll also want to ensure the platform provides templates that have been optimized for viewing across multiple types of devices.

Choose a platform that supports search engine optimization (SEO) best practices. This will help enhance your brand's visibility through search engine results and will help your educational content reach a wider audience.

You will also want to understand the cost structure offered by each platform, including subscription fees, transaction fees, and any additional associated costs. Consider how these costs align with your budget. Be sure to factor into your consideration any additional revenue that you expect to retain by selling direct to customers through your website instead of paying transaction fees to third-party e-commerce providers like eBay or Etsy.

You should also research user reviews and testimonials for insights into the experiences of other users. Pay attention to feedback related to ease of use, customer support, and the platform's performance and overall reliability.

Finally, if available, take advantage of free trial periods offered by platforms. This allows you to test the platform's features and functionality before making a long-term commitment.

15 ROOTING A PRESENCE: WEBSITE DESIGN MEETS MARKETING STRATEGY

With her website up and functional, Lily turned her attention back to her marketing plan and reviewed the activities she identified that would help her convert her eBay and Etsy buyers into loyal customers who would purchase directly through Lily's website in the future.

It was time to strengthen her brand presence when interacting with potential customers. She updated her social media profiles to include her new logo. She made similar updates to her eBay and Etsy shop profiles by improving her profiles on both platforms to better represent her brand.

She wanted her customers to feel connected to her brand and have a consistent experience with every interaction they had with Houseplant Roots. Lily carefully considered the experience her customers would have unboxing their new plants and carried her new brand identity all the way through to her packaging. She ordered the branded rubber stamps and stickers that she had identified as low-cost ways to strengthen her brand presence on her packaging. This helped her avoid needing to purchase costly custom printed boxes.

She meticulously carried through this focus to the materials that would accompany each plant and updated everything she sent along with her plants, such as plant care sheets, plant tags and thank you notes, modifying them to visually reflect her brand and encourage her eBay and Etsy buyers to visit her new website. Her package inserts were now beautiful and told a cohesive story about her brand. They also included a compelling call-to-action encouraging customers to visit her website for exclusive deals, a wider selection of plants, and plant care advice. She used functionality available on Shopify to create a discount code for her website that would apply a 10% discount to purchases. She provided her new customers with this discount code and a QR code to make it easy for them to access her website using their smartphone.

She was proud of her brand's new cohesive look and feel and eager to monitor website traffic and watch visits begin to trickle in.

She also realized it was time to strengthen her social media presence. She set a goal to post pictures of plants, and a plant care tip daily and she actively promoted her website to her social media followers. She also developed a plan to share behind-the-scenes content, customer testimonials, and provide special offers to her social media followers to create a sense of community and encourage direct purchases.

On her website, she offered another 10% discount off a first-time purchase, direct from her site, simply for signing up to receive her email newsletters. This would help her to build her email marketing list and stay connected with her customers in the future.

Compelling Calls-to-Action

If you plan to create your own website, having a marketing plan to drive visits to your site will be important. You can share your website's URL through many sources, including: social media, on the boxes that you ship your plants in, in your email outreach to customers, or even on signage that you might use for a booth at a market. Every interaction with customers or prospective customers is an opportunity to encourage visits to your website. By providing special deals, sharing exclusive information, or offering additional products, you can entice customers to visit your site. To spur some ideas, here are examples of compelling calls to action that can drive website visits:

- "For exclusive deals and a wider selection, visit our website and get 10% off your next purchase!"

- "Experience our full range of products and enjoy fast, direct shipping by visiting our website today."

- "Join our VIP club on our website to access to member-only discounts and special promotions!"

- "For a personalized shopping experience and top-notch customer service, shop directly on our website."

- "Discover more products and be the first to know about limited release rare plants by visiting our website and signing up for our free newsletter."

- "Scan this QR code or visit our website to unlock a special discount on your next order. Thank you for your purchase!"

- "Love our products? Follow us on social media and visit our website for insider access to new releases and exclusive offers."

- "Thank you for your purchase! As a token of our appreciation, enjoy a 15% discount on your next order when you shop directly on our website, use code [discount code]."

Expanding Potential Purchases with Complementary Plant Products

With her website up and functional, Lily felt a bit intimidated needing to stock her entire online store with her plants. But she quickly realized that with just a small amount of additional work, she could expand her product selection and offer a variety of complementary plant products. She would be careful to select only products that were a good fit for her brand.

As she brainstormed potential additional products she could source over time and add to her website, she documented ideas like, decorative planters and pots, macramé plant hangers, custom blended potting mix and soil amendments tailored to the needs of the specific types of plants her customers were purchasing from her, fertilizers and nutrients, plant care tools and accessories, like watering cans, spray bottles, pruning shears, plant misters, moisture meters, and plant stands! The ideas kept coming and Lily scribbled them all in her notebook. Lily filled 3 more pages of her notebook dreaming about the diverse range of additional products she could add.

Expanding your website to include a broader range of products beyond just your own plants is a strategic way to meet the needs of your customers while increasing revenue. With a little knowledge and planning, it is not difficult to extend your inventory to include products like plant care items and lifestyle products that might appeal to fellow plant lovers. When thinking about adding related products, you'll need to define the type of products you're interested in providing, determine where you'll source these items from and develop a plan for shipping them to your customers.

Inventory Expansion Ideas

There is a wide variety of products you might consider offering in addition to your plants. To give you some possible ideas of items your customers might be interested in adding to their plant order, we'll explore two potential product categories: plant care essentials and lifestyle merchandise. Of course, there are many other product categories you could consider; this isn't a comprehensive overview.

Your customers are visiting your website because they are interested in plants. They likely have plants or are starting their collection by buying their first plant from you – how exciting! These customers are very likely interested in not just plants, but in all the supplies that they'll need to take care of their plants. They may really appreciate a curated selection of plant care essentials offered direct through your website. These items could include stylish and functional watering cans, spray bottles, pruning shears, misters, and soil testers. Or, you might want to offer a selection of high-quality soils and fertilizers tailored to different types of plants, such as succulents, orchids, or tropical houseplants. Pots and planters can be another broad group of plant care essential products that would entice your customers; there is a wide variety of pots and planters you could consider offering, from eco-friendly materials to tech-enabled smart pots, complete with self-watering features! There are so many types of plant care essential items that your customers need, why not give them the opportunity to buy these items direct through your business?

Beyond just the plant care essentials, there is a whole world of lifestyle merchandise that your plant-loving customers would love to purchase. Just think about the possibility of offering coffee cups, tumblers and stickers with plant-themed designs or witty gardening puns. T-shirts and other apparel items present the same opportunities for you to share botanical illustrations or phrases that resonate with plant enthusiasts. Even better than the incremental revenue these types of lifestyle products offer, they can actually turn your customers into brand ambassadors who are proudly showcasing your brand's logo and motto in their daily lives.

<u>Sourcing Inventory Expansions</u>

Armed with a wish list of products you'd like to include in

your websites store, what do you do next? How will you go about obtaining these additional items to sell? The good news is that armed with a good idea of the types of products you want to offer, you have options available for sourcing this additional inventory.

Partnering with local artisans can be a great way to provide unique, high-quality items while simultaneously supporting other small businesses and your local economy. You'll also typically have greater control over product quality and the flexibility to create exclusive designs if you are working with local artisans. Networking at local craft fairs and artisan markets or searching online marketplaces that are dedicated to handmade goods are great places to find these partners. From there, simply introduce yourself, and share that you'd love to offer their products for sale through your website. In most cases, they'll be delighted to have another avenue for selling their items. You'll simply have to work out the payment structure and whether you'll purchase a certain number of items in advance at a wholesale rate, or whether you'll sell their items on a consignment basis through your platform.

For basic plant care items and generic lifestyle merchandise, wholesale suppliers might be your most cost-effective way to stock up on inventory. Trade shows, online wholesale directories, and forums can be valuable resources for finding reputable suppliers. When selecting a supplier, consider factors such as minimum order quantities, shipping costs, and whether you might have an option to customize the products with your branding.

Dropshipping Additional Merchandise

Okay, this all sounds great, but what about the hassle of storing and shipping these additional products, all in addition to your existing plants? Well, of course, it is an option to purchase in bulk, store items and ship them yourself, and in some cases, this might make sense for you to do. But it's not the only way!

Dropshipping is another convenient option for online businesses that are interested in expanding their product range without holding physical inventory. This model involves partnering with suppliers who fulfill this portion of your customer's order directly, sending the product to customers on your behalf. While dropshipping offers lower upfront costs and is easy to scale, it's important to ensure product quality and reliability of the partner meeting shipping times.

Expanding your online website to include related plant care items and lifestyle merchandise not only diversifies your product offering and helps you fill your store, but also enhances the overall customer experience. By carefully selecting inventory that resonates with plant enthusiasts and sourcing products through reliable channels, this is a viable path to grow a brand and nurture a loyal customer base.

Nurturing an Audience with an Email Newsletter

Continuing to hone her focus on driving website traffic and retaining lifelong customers, Lily began plotting to send out regular email newsletters. She didn't want to send out just any old newsletter, she wanted it to be engaging and value packed. She wanted it to be email that her customers would actually open.

Managing a newsletter alongside her day job and growing business would be additional work. To be successful, she would need to have a game plan. She began brainstorming content ideas, and decided early on that she would meticulously plan her content ahead of time. Each newsletter would be filled with helpful tips on plant care, intriguing stories about her plant adventures, sneak peeks into her latest plant arrivals and exclusive deals. By planning her content well in advance, she won't be under constant stress to write content. She'll be able to deliver a consistent experience to her audience and keep them engaged and informed.

To further ease the workload, Lily decides she will outsource certain aspects of her newsletter production, like graphic design, content editing and possibly even some of the necessary writing. This will allow her to focus on what she does best: nurturing plants and customer relationships. With Lily's dedication and a sprinkle of plant-loving charm, her newsletter is on its way to becoming as lush and thriving as her houseplants.

Creating an e-mail newsletter can be a very effective way for a houseplant seller to nurture their audience and generate future sales. With a little planning, it's possible to create engaging and valuable e-mail newsletter content.

If this is something you're interested in exploring with your own houseplant business. You'll want to begin by defining the purpose of the newsletter. Will you provide educational content about plant care, offer exclusive promotions or share new product arrivals? Maybe your focus will be on providing tips and inspiration for incorporating houseplants into home décor. Understanding the purpose will help guide your content development and ensure it resonates with your audience and what you are hoping to accomplish.

It almost goes without saying, but you'll need to build a subscriber list. You can encourage website visitors, social media followers, and customers to subscribe to receive your newsletter. You can offer discounts to website visitors who provide their email address and subscribe to receive your content. There are plenty of ways to gather a list of email subscribers and this will be crucial to the success of your newsletter.

Creating valuable content should be your top priority. Fortunately, in the world of houseplants there is no shortage of topics your newsletter could address! You could include tips on plant care, seasonal plant care reminders, DIY planting projects, tutorials on repotting plants, inspirational houseplant home decor ideas, customer success stories and so much more! Your content should be informative, engaging, and tailored to the interests of your audience.

Another thing to consider is that personalization can significantly enhance the effectiveness of a newsletter. You could accomplish this by segmenting your subscriber list based on factors such as purchase history, plant interests, or geographic location, and then tailor the content to each segment. Personalized recommendations might include relevant seasonal considerations for plant care based on where each subscriber lives. Or, content curated for plant experts, or content focused on beginners. Personalization keeps your content relevant and can make the newsletter more impactful for each subscriber.

Consider including exclusive offers and promotions to generate future sales. Your subscribers may be more inclined to make a future purchase if they feel they're receiving special treatment or access to deals that are not available to the public.

Your subject line is probably as important as the actual newsletter content. Remember, your subscribers are probably receiving a lot of email. To increase the odds that your email will be opened, you'll need to clearly and succinctly answer your audience's core question, "What's in it for me?" Creating engaging subject lines for your email newsletter is crucial to capture your audience's attention. Here are some creative suggestions designed to entice your subscribers to open the email and learn more:

- "Unearth New Arrivals: Exclusive Plants Inside!"

- "Transform Your Space: Must-Have Plants for Your Home"

- "Green Thumb Secrets: Tips & Tricks for Lush Plants"

- "Bloom & Grow: Save Big on This Week's Picks"

- "Invite Nature In: Discover the Perfect Plants for Your Home Office"

- "Rare Finds Alert: Limited Stock on Exotic Plants"

- "Eco-Chic Living: Sustainable Plant Accessories Just In"

- "Join Our Green Community: Events, Workshops, and More!"

- "Your Plant Wishlist: Back in Stock Favorites!"

- "From Our Garden to Yours: Personal Picks by Our Experts"

These subject lines are designed to cater to a variety of interests and intentions, encouraging your subscribers to engage with your content and explore your offerings further.

If you do try your hand at an email newsletter, consistency is key! Communicate consistently to nurture and engage the audience. You should consider establishing a regular schedule for sending out newsletters, whether it's weekly, biweekly, or monthly, and then stick to it. Consistency helps build anticipation and keeps your audience engaged.

It didn't take long for Lily to begin seeing visits to her. She was ecstatic the first time she made a direct sale through her website and couldn't help but pull out a calculator and compare the benefit of that sale to selling on eBay or Etsy. She knew that she'd retain more profit by selling directly, and she was surprised to see this was still the case – even though the customer used one of her discount codes!

Lily was actually able to offer her customers a lower price while still retaining more profit herself, a true win-win! When selling direct from her website, she didn't have to pay eBay or Etsy a portion of her sale in transaction and listing fees.

But at the same time, Lily also saw the value that eBay and Etsy offer to her brand. These large e-commerce platforms allowed her to continue to attract brand new customers. This gave her opportunities to engage with new customers and through her ongoing marketing efforts to, hopefully, convert many of these customers to be purchasers direct from her website in the future. Etsy and eBay appeal to a very large customer base and remain important sales channels for Lily. While she makes more for every sale made on her website, she has come to view the reduced profit she receives through Etsy and eBay as the cost of being able to market to, and potentially, acquire a new, lifelong customer. She continues to test her calls to action and refine her messages to encourage more of her eBay and Etsy customers to convert to buying plants directly from Lily in the future.

16 TURNING NEW LEAVES: LEARNING TO PIVOT

Lily was flying through her goals, having developed her marketing plan, launched a website, and she now was actively executing tactics from her marketing plan to drive visitors to her website. Each strategy, from social media campaigns to her email newsletter, was a seed sown that she was confident would one day blossom. She thought of the process she went through to create her marketing plan as being akin to plotting a garden—figuring out what would grow best and where.

The launch of her website was both a pinnacle moment and yet another starting line. The digital storefront was her open sign to the world and seeing her website go live gave her an energizing burst that fueled her through fatigue.

However, updating all her marketing collateral to match her new online identity had been a heavy lift. Lily found herself juggling this push of activity with a life that was already full. Her weekdays were occupied by the steady rhythm of her day job and her evenings were a nightly flurry of propagating plants, transplanting plants, packaging them for shipping, posting new listings and responding to customer inquiries. On Saturdays, the farmers' market was her stage, where she would connect with local customers face-to-face. Each night of the week, her evenings were lit by her laptop's glow, and the clacking sound of her keyboard. It was a trying time – Lily was stretched thin.

But she was also seeing results. Her marketing efforts were slowly turning into engagement with her content and driving visits to her website. Website visits were turning into profitable sales. Her business's growth was incremental, like the slow unfurling of a new leaf on a plant, but it was there. It was an intense and demanding period of her life, a test of endurance and faith in the vision she had for her business. Yet, Lily remained confident that with time and tenacity, her efforts would yield success.

She thought of all this and more during one exhausted Thursday night as she lay in bed, somehow too tired to sleep. She told herself that the following day after working her day job, she would tackle that next goal: building a subscription service and then she'd get ready for Saturday's farmers' market.

After a restless night, in the quiet light of early morning, while the world was still waking up, Lily sat with her steaming cup of tea, completing her daily social media business posts, and scrolling through her feeds. It was part of her daily ritual, searching for inspiration, trends, and opportunities in the online plant community. And that day, her routine browsing would lead her to an unexpected treasure.

A local post on Facebook Marketplace caught her eye—a hastily typed request from the family of a plant enthusiast who had recently passed away. The message was simple: they needed to clear out the house quickly to prepare it for sale and were overwhelmed by the sheer number of plants that were filling every corner of the home. The plants, they said, were free to anyone willing to take all of them.

Lily's heart raced. She saw a couple grainy pictures in the posting and could tell how well cared for the plants were. There were so many plants, she felt certain this collection likely included plant types that she didn't already own and could even include rare specimens! She picked up the phone without hesitation and dialed the number listed in the ad. A tired voice on the other end confirmed that the plants were still available and expressed a sense of urgency in their disposition.

Acting swiftly, Lily called her boss and said she needed to take the day off. Her boss was understanding, as this was something Lily rarely, if ever, had done. From there, Lily rented a small moving truck. As she drove to the address given, she felt a poignant respect for the departed gardener whose legacy she was about to inherit. Upon arrival, she was greeted by a somber family grateful to see someone who recognized the value of what their loved one had so treasured.

The house was a plant lover's paradise. Lily walked through the rooms, and her every breath was filled with the earthy scent of soil and leaves. She carefully began the process of loading the plants into boxes (something she was at this point very skilled at doing) and moving them into her rental truck.

Seeing her enthusiasm and the care with which she handled the plants, the family offered Lily additional supplies that they found in the greenhouse: a high-quality grow light, an assortment of pots, bags of soil, and various amendments—all the tools a plant lover could wish for.

Lily was touched by their generosity and promised to nurture and propagate the plants so that they could fill many more homes. Her drive back home to her apartment was quiet and contemplative, as she thought of the responsibility she now had.

Back at home, Lily began bringing her new plants in one by one, being sure to keep them separate from her existing plants, as part of her bio-security quarantine process. She marveled at the diversity and the health of her new plants. Among them were exotic aroids, flowering cacti, and a variety of succulents along with some amazing, variegated specimens that she knew her customers would simply adore. Some were plants she had never seen before, except on the pages of her plant encyclopedia.

Lily posted behind the scenes pictures to her social media that showed her moving truck filled with boxes of plants, pictures showing the chaotic scene in her apartment – every surface filled with plants and boxes of more plants covering the floor. She also included a couple pictures that showcased certain plant specimens she was especially excited about. This created immediate interest and engagement with her posts, and she quickly saw her number of followers tick up. She started receiving inquiries about whether she would sell some of the plants as is. She shared that she planned to learn about these plants first, and she was hopeful that new and rare plant cuttings could be coming soon. She was excited to see that her initial posts appeared to be building excitement with her customers, and she was eager to bring them along on this journey of learning how to care for each of these plants.

Lily took to her website, where she posted pictures and wrote a heartfelt blog post sharing the story of how these plants came into her care. She pledged to make sure that her plant enthusiast customers would soon be able to help sustain and grow the heritage of the departed gardener's collection.

This unanticipated boon enhanced Lily's collection significantly and strengthened her bonds in the plant community. It reminded her that every plant had a backstory and a life cycle that went beyond the straightforward exchange of goods for cash. She was now a gardener of legacies and a curator of shared passion.

Her enthusiasm had been rekindled by this encounter, and the next morning she was more invested in her business than ever before as she went to the farmers' market.

You may recall that Lily's big plan was to begin focusing on her subscription service after building her initial website and marketing plan. But this windfall of new plants demanded that she be flexible and modify her plan. She remembered that when she was building her business plan, she had temporarily shelved the idea of building out a rare and exotic plant collection that would target plant collectors. But having happened upon several species perfect for exactly this venture, for only the cost of renting a moving truck for the day, Lily knew she needed to adjust her plan.

She decided to focus on her new collection of plants and pause work on her subscription service. She would first work to identify each plant in her new collection. This would enable her to research its needs and make sure she was providing it an optimal growing environment. Through her research she would also learn how to propagate each new plant species.

Lily would document her progress through social media and on her website. She would use this initial activity to continue building excitement and gauging her customer's interest in each new species. She would even look to her followers for their help identifying certain types of plants! This activity would also help her build deep and meaningful content for her website.

Lily's life had taken on a new rhythm, a cadence marked by the ebb and flow of growth and care that came with the inheritance of the plant collector's green legacy and learning to manage the nuanced care that some of the plants required. The plants she had brought into her home were more than just botanical specimens; they were living memorials, each leaf and stem a testament to a fellow gardener's love and devotion.

Lily made it her mission to not only maintain the health of these plants but to understand their histories, their preferences and the little quirks that made each one unique. After identifying each plant and learning about its environmental needs, Lily would post pictures of the plant to her website and carefully document her learnings and observations. Her content went deeper than the plant's basic care needs; Lily wove into each paragraph the narrative of the plant's history and told a story about how plants can connect people through time and space. With each post, she honored the history of the plant, and ensured that the love their previous caretaker had obviously poured into them continued to resonate.

Under Lily's care, the plants settled into their new home, and soon exotic aroids unfurled new, glossy leaves, and flowering cacti burst into vibrant blooms. All the while, succulents multiplied and their offsets spilled over the edges of their pots. The grow light the family had given Lily hummed throughout the days and into the nights, bathing the plants in a spectrum of light perfectly tailored to their needs.

Lily's thoughtfully crafted website and social media content brought her droves of new followers and website visitors. Some came for the storytelling that connected plants and history, others came waiting for the day Lily would offer propagations for certain rare plants, and along the way, many purchased from Lily's shop.

Lily became adept at propagating each new type of plant, carefully tending to the offspring of the original collection. Cuttings were rooted and pups were separated. These 'children' of the collector's plants were lovingly nurtured until they, too, were strong enough to stand on their own. She started selling the offspring, now robust young plants, exclusively through her website and was delighted to ship them to fellow plant lovers far and wide.

With each sale, she included a note about the plant's lineage, and a brief story about how plants are a living testament to the love and care a plant caretaker gives, and how this love lives on through these green beings. Customers were not just buying a plant; they were adopting a piece of history, becoming part of a narrative that held the promise to stretch beyond their own lives. The plants connected people, creating a community of individuals who shared a piece of the late collector's spirit. Lily felt a sense of fulfillment, knowing that the love for plants she shared with the collector was branching out, touching lives, and beautifying corners of the world she would never see.

In her quiet moments, when she sat among the greenery that filled her home, Lily felt a profound connection to the cycle of life. She knew that if she continued to care for these plants, to propagate them and share them, the collector's passion would never fade, and neither would hers. It was a legacy written in chlorophyll, in the whispers of leaves, and in the earthy scent of soil—a legacy that would grow and flourish as long as there were hands to tend plants and hearts to appreciate the quiet joy they bring.

A Lesson in Market Awareness, Respect and Passon

Market Awareness

It was only through her diligent engagement in her local plant market that Lily positioned herself to recognize and embrace unique opportunities. The lesson for all aspiring plant entrepreneurs is that attentiveness to market trends matters. Staying engaged in community forums and other networks can open you up to a world of possible opportunities that would otherwise fly by, unseen.

Lily's story of acquiring this additional plant collection underscores the importance of staying informed and connected to capitalize on potential prospects that may arise. Be aware of your current market and stay current with the latest happenings in your community.

Storytelling a Source of Brand Enrichment

Lily's respect for the plants' history and the previous owner's dedication transformed her business into more than just a commercial venture. It became a conduit for preserving legacy.

By valuing the stories and the sentimental worth of the plants, she enriched her life, and added depth and meaning to her work. This reverence elevated her practice from mere cultivation to stewardship.

Lily's genuine care for the plants and their back story resonated with her customers, creating a bond that went beyond the transaction of a sale. It was her emotional investment that drew people to her business.

In essence, Lily's experience with the collector's plants teaches us that while professional acumen can open doors to opportunities, it is the heart-led respect for one's work and the narratives that are entwined with it that truly enrich a business endeavor.

So, whether it's through a similar reverence for history or finding a different way to derive deep emotional connection to your customers, storytelling matters. Passion and authenticity build loyalty and trust. Engaging your audience with a narrative will position you to transcend transactional sales. Whether it's a story about your brand, or a story about your plants, a strong purpose-led message can add value to each sale.

17 GROWING PAINS BEGIN AND PARTNERSHIPS FORM

Lily's apartment had transformed into an absolute jungle, a testimony to her thriving plant business. Every nook and cranny reflected her ambition, with pots and planters crowding the floor, macramé hangers swaying gently from the ceiling, and nearly every surface covered with plants in various stages of growth.

Her new collection of exotic plants and their propagations had begun to outgrow the confines of her living space. Although she reveled in the financial rewards her hard work was bringing, the creeping realization that she needed more space, and with it more expense, was undeniable.

The next weekend at the farmers' market, Lily asked Herb how he kept up with producing inventory to sell at the market and online, alongside maintaining his living space. She shared her amazing story of acquiring a large new array of plants and her excitement at watching her business grow. Their mutual appreciation for nature's beauty sparked a connection, and soon, Herb was standing amidst the leafy abundance of Lily's cramped apartment for conversation about their businesses.

During this first fateful visit, Herb struggled to navigate his way around Lily's plants. An accidental misstep resulted in a glass jar of cuttings falling to the floor with a shatter. Herb felt horrible and apologized profusely, as Lily swept up the broken glass and assured him it was alright.

That night, as Herb headed home, his mind whirred with ideas to help Lily maximize space in her apartment. He had an idea and with a spark of inspiration, set to work on a concept that would blend his craftsmanship in woodworking with Lily's love for propagating plants.

At the farmers' market the following weekend, Herb gave Lily two concept pieces—both elegant, wall-mounted wood artwork designed to hold plant cuttings on the wall, off the surface of countertops and in a visually stunning display. Lily loved them! The pieces were not just functional, they were art, and they offered the promise of helping her reclaim some of her living space in the most beautiful way.

She hung Herb's initial creations on her wall and posted pictures to her social media channels. The interest was immediate. Her followers were also plant enthusiasts, many of whom propagated plants on their own, and they wanted to buy their own plant propagation wall art! Lily called Herb and her first business partnership was officially born. She began to offer Herb's woodworking pieces on her website and his items were a hit.

Herb also brought his new creations to the farmers' market the following Saturday, and he moved his booth right near Lily's. The collaboration of jointly showcasing their inventory was a hit. They realized that the following weekend they could reduce their operating expenses by selling jointly from a single booth in future markets!

Herb's woodworking pieces became the perfect complement to Lily's lush plants, each sale a testament to the power of creativity and collaboration.

Strategic Partnerships to Grow Your Business

Strategic partnerships are a powerful tool for businesses who are looking to expand into new markets. Partnerships come in various forms, such as alliances with other companies, collaborations with influencers or even joint ventures.

To be successful, partners need aligned goals, clear communication, and a mutual understanding of what each brings to the table. Both businesses can maintain their own identities and value propositions while working together to create synergy. A well-executed strategic partnership can lead to growth that neither partner could achieve alone.

Let's look at just a couple ways strategic partnerships can propel small businesses.

Reaching New Markets

Partnerships can open doors to markets that might otherwise be difficult or impossible to reach. This can help a company expand their revenue sources.

Businesses can help one another reach new audiences by cross-promoting products or services, which can increase sales and customer loyalty for both companies.

Additionally, each company in this type of partnership can benefit from the reputation and brand of its partner. This can lead to increased visibility among the partner's customer base.

In Lily and Herb's case, by marketing Herb's products to Lily's customers, Herb is able to reach an audience of plant customers who would be unlikely to otherwise visit Herb's woodworking website.

Shared Resources

Partners can share resources like facilities, technology, distribution channels, customer bases and expertise. This can reduce costs – an important benefit, especially to small business owners.

For example, Lily and Herb discovered that through a partnership they're able to reduce their farmers' market booth fees by joining forces and selling out of a single booth.

Innovation

Collaboration can lead to innovation as partners combine their strengths and perspectives to create new products or services.

In Herb's example, the problem that he encountered when knocking over one of Lily's cutting jars inspired him to use his woodworking skills and create a wall mounted, decorative holder for plant cuttings.

18 GREEN SPACES: THE NEXT BIG EXPANSION

Lily's journey from houseplant lover to a thriving entrepreneur had expanded and morphed over time and for the most part, she had been able to adapt her space and life based on her business's needs. Houseplant Roots LLC began in just the corner of her living room, and for her first year this served her well, with her living room being the perfect nursery for her plant cuttings and her young business.

As demand grew, Lily began to see that her existing living room space could no longer contain her full aspirations. Although Herb's woodworking pieces allowed her to hang some of her cuttings on her walls instead of cluttering her countertops, her apartment remained crowded. Between the supplies she used to ship her houseplants and cuttings, the empty pots, bags of soil and her houseplant collection which had itself grown, Lily sometimes felt like there was little room left for her.

She also missed being able to spend time with her friends. She wanted to be able to spend her days focusing on her business and her evenings and weekends with friends and family doing other activities. But instead, she spent her days commuting to her day job, working behind a desk for someone else, only to then need to commute back home. Her focus during her nights and weekends was on her business. The success her business was achieving was a blessing, but it left little room for anything else.

Lily began wondering what options she had available. She needed more space, more time, and the ability to fully prioritize her days. Could she quit her day job and focus on Houseplant Roots LLC full-time, she wondered? What could she do about her limited space? Would it be possible for her to buy property with enough space to be able to further grow her business? These questions and more filled her mind.

Lily knew these were big decisions; she wanted to be certain the choices she made would set her up for success in her business's future growth and give her more options in her personal life. Her next steps would require careful planning and a strategic approach to navigate a successful transition to both full-time entrepreneurship and property ownership.

Lily began examining her revenue from Houseplant Roots LLC. To transition to work for her business exclusively, she would need a consistent and stable income that she could rely on. She did appreciate the security her day job offered and would need to be certain she was ready before making a drastic change.

In just her first year of business, Lily had built a financial cushion with her side business. She had kept her expenses low and, while she did reinvest in her business to propel its growth, she had also managed to build a reserve. Based on her current expenses, she estimated that she had funds to cover her personal and business expenses for about five to six months, and perhaps longer if she were to reduce expenses. If she left paid employment, maintaining a reserve would be especially important to help navigate seasonal ebbs and flows she had observed in her business revenue.

Lily also thought about the growth potential of her business. With her approach of selling houseplants at the farmers' market, on her own website and through eBay and Etsy, she was barely able to keep up with orders. With more time and space, Lily believed she would be able to produce more, and she felt confident that increased production would translate directly to increased sales. Being able to dedicate more time to her business could significantly increase her revenue and open up new opportunities.

Lily also saw that there were clear benefits to maintaining paid employment. The consistent, predictable income she received from her salaried job allowed her the freedom to grow Houseplant Roots LLC. She had been able to strategically reinvest in her business, in large part because she hadn't been funding her life with revenue from her business. If she were to quit her paid employment, she would need to carefully manage her business's cash flow, and perhaps take fewer risks.

Lily also received health insurance from her day job. This was something else to consider. If she left her job, she would need to purchase health insurance directly and she was concerned that this could be costly.

Finally, as Lily thought about potentially buying a property where she would have space to grow her business, she learned more about what would be needed to apply for a mortgage. Employment stability can be a key factor in a mortgage decision, so leaving her day job could make it more difficult for her to purchase a property now or in the future.

Ultimately, Lily realized what she wanted, and she knew that she needed a plan to achieve her vision. Lily wanted to leave her day job to focus on Houseplant Roots LLC full-time, and she needed space to be able to expand her plant business.

She recognized that it may be advantageous for her to secure a mortgage before leaving her day job. She contacted a real estate agent, applied for mortgage preapproval, and started browsing property listings.

Her plan was to use some of her current savings to fund her downpayment. After securing a property, she would retain her day job for a period of time to rebuild her savings cushion.

At that point, she would talk to her boss and attempt to transition her full-time employment to part-time. She figured that by phasing her transition, and gradually reducing the time she spent at her day job she would be able to take steps to scale up her business. This approach would minimize her financial risk and help ensure a smoother transition.

She also realized that searching for a property would be an additional drain on her already limited time, not to mention the stress that a move would mean. Lily was already feeling overwhelmed with her current responsibilities. She consulted with Herb and other business owners she had met at Small Business Association events and shared how she was feeling and what she hoped to accomplish. She asked for their guidance on how to navigate this transition.

A theme she heard from nearly everyone she spoke with was that in *order to balance both her day job and growing business while navigating a property purchase and a move, Lily would need a deliberate time management strategy. She took this advice and built a detailed calendar for herself. She scheduled her time across every hour of the day to ensure she was effectively allocating time and maximizing her productivity.*

Lily also heard that developing a detailed financial plan that would account for potential fluctuations in her houseplant business income would help her understand her options and prepare for the future. She began building a plan to encompass her personal expenses, business investments, and anticipated property-related costs. She would need to adhere closely to this plan.

Those she spoke with also reminded Lily how important it would be for her to build a support network. She already had a great start, and she made a list in her notebook titled "Support Networks." These are the people she would turn to when she was overwhelmed, to seek their guidance, insights, and emotional support during the transition.

The winds of fortune blew kindly on Lily, and before long, she found herself the owner of a house in the countryside, with enough land to build her very own greenhouse.

As she prepared for her big move, Lily spent time considering how she would set up both her business and personal spaces. She began packing up her apartment and noted the types of activities she conducted for her business. There was a need for an area for her plants to grow and an area for propagating and cultivating her plants. She noted that she would need a potting area where she could transplant her young pots, and she needed space to stage items that she would take to the farmers' market, and of course she needed to dedicate space to packaging and shipping the plants and cuttings that she sold online.

She outlined the types of activities she would complete and thought through how to set her business up for efficient operations at her new home.

She also researched her options for building a greenhouse. She reflected on how her space requirements had changed over time. Of course, she could have chosen to maintain her houseplant business as a small business selling cuttings or plants. The plants she already had provided her with everything she needed to get started. Jumping in had been as straightforward as taking a cutting from an existing plant. She had come a long way with a growing business that now allowed her to consider dedicated space for each activity!

It was an exciting problem to have. Lily knew that selecting the right space to grow her plants would directly affect their health, the potential scale of her future operations, and ultimately the success of her business.

As Lily began thinking about all the activities she undertook for her business and planning how she would need to use her space, she also began researching greenhouse options. A greenhouse would allow her to accommodate a larger number of plants, increasing potential revenue. A greenhouse would also extend her outdoor growing season and give her the ability to create an ideal growing environment for a variety of plants.

Of course, this type of infrastructure would require significant up-front costs. A greenhouse would require regular ongoing maintenance.

However, for her business to grow further, she would need as much growing space as possible to keep up with customer demand. She also believed that by adding a greenhouse she would be better prepared to manage seasonal fluctuations in sales by providing her with a controlled environment for year-round production. It might even allow her to expand her product range to include a wider variety of plants or offer seasonal crops like tulips in the spring and mums in the fall.

As she looked over her greenhouse type and size options, she quickly found drastic price variations. There were smaller hobby greenhouses, massive commercial greenhouse options, and everything in between. There would be a cost to purchase her greenhouse and cost to have it installed, and these business expenses needed to be planned for.

She once again found herself seeking out guidance from her local Small Business Association. She was delighted when they were able to connect her with lenders and agricultural resources in the area. She learned there were several financial options available to her. These weren't just limited to loans, either; there were also grants and incentives available for greenhouse construction and for the use of energy efficient technologies.

Ultimately, Lily applied for local energy efficiency grants that would help her afford energy efficient greenhouse options. The additional financial assistance, coupled with the long-term financial benefit of *energy efficient options felt like the right long-term approach for her business's success.*

Scaling Your Operations

If you are thinking about scaling a houseplant business and exploring whether a greenhouse is right for you, conduct a cost-benefit analysis to ensure that the potential increase in revenue justifies the initial investment and the ongoing maintenance.

You might want to start with a small or medium-sized greenhouse to learn about ways to manage costs and to learn some of the complexities before building a larger greenhouse.

Of course, you do not have to have a greenhouse, or even future visions of scaling up to a greenhouse, in order to run a successful houseplant side hustle. There are many options available to use space you already have or to dedicate additional space in your home your business.

Using Existing Space to Scale Up

Starting small with just existing space in your home minimizes start-up costs since there's no need to invest in additional space or structures. It's easy to monitor and care for plants that are already in your living space and this might not be any additional work beyond what you are already doing to care for your plants.

Of course, you'll want to plan where to locate plants based on their light and temperature requirements. If you plan to use your existing living space for your plants, it's important to choose plants that thrive in the conditions of your home.

While it's great to start where you are, over time, leveraging your existing living space might restrict your ability to grow your business. And, for some of us, our living space might not provide ideal light or temperature conditions, or our conditions may vary widely and hinder plant growth. Seasonal changes in your living space could be a challenge if you're interested in growing certain plant species, as natural shifts in light and temperature can be problematic.

Simple Adjustments to Better Meet the Needs of Plants

Luckily, even if your existing living space is problematic for the type or quantity of plants you want to grow, there are many options available to help you create an environment for plants to thrive. Indoor grow lights mounted to a sturdy shelf can help meet plants' light requirements if your natural lighting is inadequate. You also may have unused space such as a spare bedroom where you may be able to house more plants, while potentially also maintaining more precise environmental control over factors such as temperature, lighting and humidity.

Adding grow lights for plants offers you the ability to precisely control the amount of light and type of light your plants receive. With grow lights, you can cultivate plants regardless of natural light availability. Humidifiers allow you to add humidity to a room. Dehumidifiers reduce the humidity in a room. Heaters can add heat, while air conditioners or swamp coolers may be an option for cooling a space that is too warm on its own.

Of course, it's always possible to start small with a few shelves in a dedicated space and expand as your demand grows. Be sure to consider the initial cost of any special equipment you plan to use, along with potential increases in electricity consumption.

No matter where you start, there's always the potential to scale your houseplant side hustle. Starting with just a windowsill, over time dedicating shelf space, followed by expanding to a spare bedroom, and potentially moving all the way up to a full-scale greenhouse, like Lily, offers a clear path to scaling a houseplant side hustle. Each step of the way, you'll learn more about plant care, business operations, and customer preferences, which will inform your decisions and strategies for growth.

19 BRANCHING OUT: SUBSCRIPTION SERVICE MODEL

Buying her property and adding her greenhouse were significant steps that marked the beginning of an exciting new chapter for Lily, one that she hoped would eventually allow her to leave her full-time job and immerse herself completely in her growing business.

Lily wanted to find ways to help her balance the ebbs and flows of income that come with running a small business. If she were able to predict revenue more accurately for her business, she would feel more prepared to begin phasing out her day job.

As she thought through ways to make her houseplant income more stable and predictable, she remembered her previous plan to start a subscription service for plants. She had temporarily put this on hold when she chose to pivot and adjust her priorities to take advantage of the opportunity she came across to acquire additional plants, which allowed her to begin to explore a more rare and exotic plant line. Lily was excited to now be in a position to revisit the idea of a subscription service.

She learned that subscription service models are a succession selling strategy. They are aimed at developing a continuous flow of products to customers. Lily believed a subscription service offering could revolutionize her business model.

The subscription service she envisioned would offer a range of options to suit different customers' needs. From monthly deliveries of unique, *easy-to-care-for houseplants to three or six-month subscription lines focused on unique plant types like cactuses of the desert or plants renowned for healing capabilities–* her mind was spinning! There were so many options that would allow her to cater to a broad spectrum of plant lovers and gift givers. This model would not only ensure a steady income stream but would also allow Lily to predict her inventory requirements with better accuracy and enable her to optimize her new greenhouse space.

Lily intended to start small, testing the waters with a limited number of subscriptions to gauge customer interest and refine her service approach. As the subscription model gained traction, she would gradually reduce her hours at her full-time job, transitioning to part-time work. This phased approach was strategic, providing her with a financial safety net to grow her business while alleviating some of the immediate financial pressure.

Of course, Lily began her subscription service plan by creating a SMART goal for herself. She spent time crafting this goal to make sure it was focused on delivering the results that would matter the most. In her notebook, she wrote:

> *"Specific: I will launch a houseplant subscription service to provide customers with a unique, easy-to-care-for plant each month.*
>
> *Measurable: I will acquire 100 subscribers within the first three months of launching this service.*
>
> *Achievable: I will achieve this by utilizing my new greenhouse space to cultivate a diverse range of houseplants, and to ensure a steady supply that is planned in advance for the subscription service. I will implement marketing strategies, including promotions to my social media and newsletter, and I'll add signage at my farmers' market booth to attract subscribers.*
>
> *Relevant: This subscription service directly aligns with my objective of creating a consistent and predictable income stream*

and will help me reach my goals of transitioning gradually from my full-time job to focus solely on my plant business.

Time-Bound: I will launch the subscription service by the first of next month, with the goal of reaching 100 subscribers by end of month, three months later."

Lily reflected on her goal and felt confident that she had outlined a clear, focused target for her subscription service, and that it encompassed all the key elements she needed to consider for successful implementation and growth of her vision.

And sure enough, as Lily identified the initial plants she would offer through this service and built her plan to ensure she had adequate cuttings and young plants to supply 100 customers with something new each month, her confidence in the approach grew. Lily began posting the offering to her social media channels and shared her new, limited availability offering through her newsletter and on her website.

Subscriptions started to come in and this new service model had officially taken root!

Her once small side hustle was once again, on a rapid growth trajectory. She was able to better predict her business's revenue each month, and she had a very clear sense of the plant inventory she needed to prepare to be ready for the months ahead.

It was time for her to make the leap, to transition to part-time employment, add additional subscription options and soon to fully leave the security of her outside job and devote herself entirely to her houseplant dream. It still felt like a risk, but for Lily, the chance to turn her passion for houseplants into a flourishing enterprise was a risk worth taking.

20 DREAMS CONTINUE TO GROW

In her new greenhouse, surrounded by plants, Lily felt a sense of accomplishment and excitement for the future. She had transformed her passion into a profession. And in doing so, she was not just selling plants, she was spreading the joy and tranquility that comes with nurturing a piece of nature in one's own home.

Lily walked the aisles, reflecting on how far she had come and how she had been able to bring so many of her ideas to life. The moment she left her paid employment to focus on her entrepreneurial venture brough her, once again, that now familiar feeling of reaching a coveted finish line to realize it was a new starting point. She was eager for the future and ready for new adventures that lay ahead. She reflected on her earliest days of first beginning to sell on eBay and Etsy, on the friendships she had forged, and mentors she gained through her farmers' market experiences and visits to the Small Business Association.

As she walked through her plants, she gazed at a leaf from one of the stunning plants she had acquired as part of the late plant collector's collection. She remembered the day she found the listing for this additional plant collection, and how the plants brought her not just new types of inventories through different varieties, but how the experience ended up helping her create content that had propelled her social media and the development of her brand. She thought about ways she could continue to expand and grow from this momentum. Her mind drifted to a potential future where maybe she would explore a plant rehoming service. It would be rooted in the act of preserving the stories of each plant's origin and the larger narrative of plants and their offspring connecting people across space and time. Lily recognized the significance that the stories behind the plants played in her success and the value of sharing these connections.

She wondered if there was an opportunity to extend her business in a way that not only honored the plants' origin stories but also created a meaningful and compassionate service for her community.

Her appreciation for the emotional value of the plants and how her customers embraced the storytelling aspect of her business had inspired her to think beyond traditional sales and consider how she could continue to bring joy and connection to people through a shared love of plants.

She envisioned a rehoming service for plants that could reflect her desire to create a lasting impact. What would this look like? How would she do it? She thought of herself sitting down with people who were moving long distances, people who were transitioning to nursing homes and others making major life changes that weren't compatible with their houseplant collection. She would offer them a fair price for their plants. She would give people an opportunity to share the memories they have about their plants, where they came from, how they've cared for the plant over the years. She will show empathy and understanding, recognizing the emotional attachment and significance of these stories. Lily will preserve their stories and share them with the new owners of the plants and their offspring.

Maye she will write personalized notes or create certificates to accompany the plants when they are rehomed, providing the new caretakers with a glimpse into the plant's history and the memories associated with it. She hopes to one day create a legacy for plants, ensuring that their origins and the memories attached to them continue to thrive for years to come.

Plant Your Own Hustle

The world of houseplants is not just a market; it's a canvas of endless possibilities, vibrant with opportunities and ripe for innovation. The market for houseplants is robust and expanding, fueled by a growing interest in green living and interior décor. This growth opens up a multitude of paths for success, each unique and promising in its own right.

Remember, there is no single route to success in this venture. The beauty of the houseplant business lies in its expansive diversity. Whether you find your niche in rare and exotic plants, focus on sustainable and organic growth methods, or excel in creating unique plant-based products, there is space for you in this industry. The key is to identify what resonates with you and your target audience, and to build your business and story around that.

Moreover, the variety of sales channels available today – from online platforms and social media to local markets and pop-up events – means you can reach customers in so many ways. Each channel brings its own advantages and caters to different segments of the market. This versatility allows you to tailor a business model to what works best for you, whether it's purely an online presence, a community-focused approach, or a blend of channels.

Success in the houseplant business can take many forms. For some, it might be the satisfaction of nurturing a small but loyal customer base. For others, it could be the thrill of seeing their brand recognized nationally. Success could also mean the ability to support environmental causes or contribute to community well-being. Whatever your definition of success is, it is possible to create in this ever-evolving market.

Take a stroll through digital marketplaces like eBay or Etsy and appreciate the world of plant enthusiasts who have turned their love for greenery into profitable ventures. These platforms are bustling with activity, and a quick search should provide you with any additional motivation you need. There are sellers with thousands of glowing reviews, customers celebrating their new leafy companions, and an entire community supporting small businesses. Each of these success stories is a testament to a hobby transformed into a livelihood, and each purchase is a shared piece of a personal story.

If you're so inspired, your existing houseplants are standing by waiting for you, ready to be more than just décor; they're a renewable resource that can be propagated, cultivated, and shared. By taking cuttings, nurturing them into new plants, and offering them up to the world, you can tap into a market of plant lovers yearning for that perfect piece of green to complete their collection. And remember, it's not just about the sale—it's about the story, the care tips you provide, the personal touch that comes with each plant baby grown from your own carefully tended garden.

So, as you step into this green world, carry with you the knowledge and insights from this book, but more importantly, bring your passion, creativity, and resilience. The journey of a houseplant side hustler is as rewarding as it is challenging, and your unique vision and dedication will help you unlock the special rewards it holds for you. The market is waiting, the opportunities are plentiful, and your path to success is yours to forge.

This is not a dream or a cute story. It's a call to action, an invitation to join the ranks of green-thumbed entrepreneurs who started right where you are now. With each snip and cutting placed in water to root, with every packaged plant sent to a new home, you can build a brand, a reputation, and a side hustle with potential to blossom into so much more. Your journey into plant propagation and sales could begin today, one cutting at a time, growing into a venture as robust and vibrant as the plants you love.

The beauty of this venture is just how attainable it is to start by beginning modestly. You could comfortably bring in a few hundred extra dollars a month with minimal additional effort. Even better, the "work" of this endeavor might not feel like work at all, but rather simply an expansion of a hobby you already enjoy. From there, the sky is the limit. There are an infinite number of paths you can venture down if you're interested in expanding a side hustle into something bigger.

Our hero, Lily's business model was simple yet effective. Start with what you have, grow it well, reinvest your initial profits, and gradually diversify as you learn, explore, and encounter new opportunities. With each new plant that she propagated, her skills deepened, her garden flourished, and her side hustle bloomed. Lily's story is a testament to the potential that lies in the pots and planters of any plant enthusiast willing to take that first snip and share the beauty of their growth with the world.

If you are interested in a houseplant side hustle, just like Lily, your path may meander. Don't feel like you need every piece in place in order to get started. Lily started selling plants online, then formed her legal business structure, branched out to sell at the farmers' market, and learned about how best to ship plants along the way; she shifted gears to expand her plant collection when an opportunity arose. She was well into her journey before she built a business plan, identified partnership opportunities, and built a website. Her business continues to evolve, and her dreams are still growing today. If she had waited to get started until she had built a thorough, end-to-end plan, she would have missed important opportunities and lessons along the way.

Stay close to your market, know your target niche and be open to new opportunities. Take advantage of opportunities that present themselves and be open to modifying your approach when opportunity calls.

REFERENCES

Cheng, D. (2019). *The New Plant Parent: Develop Your Green Thumb and Care for Your House-Plant Family.* Abrams.

Peerless, V. (2017). *How Not to Kill Your Houseplant: Survival Tips for the Horticulturally Challenged.* DK Publishing.

KUNR Public Radio. (2022, December 28). Houseplants boomed during the pandemic. Gen Z and Millennials say the popularity is here to stay. KUNR Public Radio. Retrieved from https://www.kunr.org

Houseplant Resource Center. (n.d.). The Plant-Crazy Generation: Why Millennials are Leading the Houseplant Trend. Houseplant Resource Center. Retrieved from https://houseplantresourcecenter.com/2021/02/the-plant-crazy-generation-why-millennials-are-leading-the-houseplant-trend/

Garden Pals. (n.d.). Houseplant Statistics in 2024 (incl. Covid & Millennials). Garden Pals. Retrieved from https://gardenpals.com/houseplant-statistics/

Royal Horticultural Society (RHS). (n.d.). Houseplants: to support human health. RHS Gardening. Retrieved from https://www.rhs.org.uk

University of Washington - Right as Rain. (n.d.). Health Benefits of Indoor Plants. Right as Rain by UW Medicine. Retrieved from https://rightasrain.uwmedicine.org

ECOgardener. (2021, September 17). Houseplant Trends: Most Popular Indoor Plants in 2024. Retrieved from https://ecogardener.com

Camille Styles. (n.d.). 2023 Indoor Plant Trends — Experts Share 7 Houseplants to Know. Retrieved from https://camillestyles.com

Arch2O. (n.d.). 9 Marvelous Houseplant Trends That Will Dominate Our Living Spaces in 2023. Retrieved from https://www.arch2o.com

ABOUT THE AUTHOR

Finn Arbor enjoys a simple life surrounded by a lively household that's a blend of family, dogs and an ever-growing assortment of barnyard friends. Finn has a keen eye for the road less traveled, and over the past several years has become somewhat of a connoisseur of unique side hustle ideas and untapped opportunities, with a constant goal of blending the essence of simple living with a passionate quest for financial freedom. Through explorations in homesteading and the joys of a home-centered life, Finn offers a refreshing perspective on making a living that's both fulfilling and fruitful with writings invite readers into a world where the good life is within reach.

Green Profits: The Budding Entrepreneur's Guide to a Houseplant Side Hustle

www.ingramcontent.com/pod-product-compliance
Lightning Source LLC
Chambersburg PA
CBHW060534100426
42743CB00009B/1532